Romantic music
A concise history

Arnold Whittall

Romantic music

A concise history
from Schubert to Sibelius

with 51 illustrations

 Thames and Hudson

Printed in Great Britain by
Alden Press, Oxford
Bound in Great Britain by
Bath Press, Bath

Contents

Preface   7

1 'Romanticism': a word and its world   9

2 Shadow and stimulus: the move away from Classicism   16

3 'A gracious, well-bred air': Romanticism in Germany before Wagner   31

4 'True passion and emotion': the Italian alternative, from Paganini to Donizetti   45

5 'Beethoven being dead . . .': Berlioz and Romanticism in France   55

6 'The scent of Paradise': Chopin's radicalism and the imagery of Romanticism   72

7 Liszt and Wagner: the high Romantic drama   81

8 'Half vulture, half phoenix': Verdi's
   Romantic synthesis   110

9 From Glinka to Grieg: crosscurrents in
   Romantic nationalism   129

10 Along the fringe: late Romantic music in
   Britain, France and America   152

11 Symphony and song: Vienna in the later
   nineteenth century   163

12 Into the twentieth century   174

   Select bibliography   185

   List of illustrations   187

   Index   189

Preface

It requires a healthy dose of Romantic bravado to add another survey to the mountain of secondary literature on this most written-about of musical phenomena. Yet it will be an important feature of this particular survey to argue that Romanticism in music is more than mere bravado – a bold and highly emotional gesture in the face of Classical traditions and conventions. Romanticism reinterpreted and also challenged the Classical coherences, embracing both an aspiration towards greater integration, and an acceptance of the fragmentary, the discontinuous. It would therefore scarcely be appropriate to offer an account that presents Romantic music as an indivisibly unified whole. My intention has been, as an enthusiast, to describe and celebrate the diversity of Romantic music; not, as a specialist, to impose a convenient but artificial unity on it.

A comprehensive history of musical life during the Romantic era would doubtless give as much emphasis to matters of social milieu, amateur and professional; performance practice; developments in instrumental design; and critical and theoretical attitudes as to the works, and lives, of a limited number of composers. My emphasis is on the music itself, on the Romantic composers generally regarded as most significant, and on the most vital structural and expressive features of the compositions they conceived. Inevitably, the reader will have no difficulty in compiling a long list of absentees – my own begins with Alkan (mentioned only in passing) and ends with Zemlinsky – but I have tried to include discussion of every composer whose absence would positively distort the narrative. Quotation in the text is confined almost entirely to the words of composers themselves and critics contemporary with them, but I have benefited greatly from the results of recent research into the period. Full details of those sources to which I am particularly indebted, and whose translations I have generally followed, appear in the Select bibliography.

1 *Ravine in the Elbsandstein Mountains, c.* 1823, by Caspar David Friedrich. Regarded by many as the quintessential Romantic artist, Friedrich created spectacular landscapes notable for their powerful evocation of supernatural and elemental forces.

CHAPTER ONE

'Romanticism': a word and its world

Gustav Mahler, in a letter to a friend of July 1894, refers to one of the most celebrated of all definitions of Romanticism. 'What Goethe says on the meaning of the terms Classical and Romantic is this: "What is Classical I call healthy, what is Romantic sick . . . Most modern work is Romantic not because it is modern but because it is weak, sickly and ill, and old work is not Classical because it is old but because it is strong, fresh, joyful and healthy. If we distinguish Classical and Romantic by these criteria, the situation is soon clarified." The inner connection between my argument and Goethe's should be obvious', Mahler adds, leaving us to assume his absolute rejection of the label 'Romantic' for anything worthwhile in music.

Many other musicians have shared Mahler's irritation at the apparent indestructibility of a term which, if Goethe is to be believed, is relevant only to art which fails to achieve the virtues of Classicism. Goethe's broadside may have been aimed at the French Romantics in particular, rather than at Romanticism in general, but it still betrays a comprehensive irritation with the term itself which has probably had an even longer and healthier history than the phenomenon it seeks to describe. If anything, that irritation is less evident today, in keeping with the current consensus that Romantic art is not so much less healthy, and therefore less valuable, than Classical art as less stable, less single-minded. It is not that Classic is good, Romantic bad, but that the virtues of both are complementary. Nevertheless, acceptance of the term in principle does not make it any the easier to define in practice. Mario Praz, in his book *The Romantic Agony*, used Keats's famous line 'Heard melodies are sweet, but those unheard are sweeter' to promote his view that the essence of Romanticism is 'that which cannot be described'; and a musician may retort that, if unheard melodies are sweeter than heard ones, undescribed unheard melodies are perhaps the sweetest – and most Romantic – of all.

Dictionaries indicate that 'Romantic' first appeared in English in 1659, that it was present in French and German by the end of the seventeenth century, and that in the eighteenth century it was linked by Dr Johnson, in appropriately rationalist vein, with such notions as 'wild' and 'fanciful'. The term had not significantly changed its meaning by the time it came to be applied regularly to music, fairly early in the nineteenth century, although the originally pejorative overtones of 'wild' and 'fanciful' were transformed into an admiring apprehension of the 'sublime' and the 'infinite'. German literary historians were the first to identify the elements of a Romantic period in the arts. For example, Novalis in 1798: 'By endowing the commonplace with a lofty significance, the ordinary with a mysterious aspect, the familiar with the merit of the unfamiliar, the finite with the appearance of infinity, I am Romanticizing'; and K. W. F. Schlegel, also in 1798, writing about Romantic poetry: 'It alone is infinite. It alone is free. Its overriding principle is that the poet's fantasy is subject to no agreed principles.' Such statements mark the beginning of the long historiography of Romanticism, of writing concerned with the term itself as much as with the works of art which exemplify it. Today, in the view of Jerome J. McGann, it is even possible to distinguish a Romantic theory of Romanticism, like that of Coleridge, which vainly aspires to reconcile its own inherent contradictions, from a non-Romantic, integrated theory of Romanticism, like Hegel's. Writers on music have always been less inclined to theorize, not least because it has never seemed plausible to regard Romantic music as a superior replacement for something inferior – the Classicism of Haydn, Mozart and Beethoven. Nevertheless, the first significant application of the word to music, in E. T. A. Hoffmann's essay of 1810 on Beethoven, describes all music, not just Beethoven's, as at least potentially Romantic: Hoffmann claims that music is 'the most Romantic of all the arts – one might even say that it alone is purely Romantic'.

Many music lovers today will certainly see the point in identifying Romantic traits in most if not all periods of musical history, especially the Baroque – in Monteverdi's *L'incoronazione di Poppea* for example, as well as in Bach's more grandiose and chromatic organ works, or Handel's more expressive arias. This book is not an account of Romanticism in this 'intrinsic' sense, but rather of the time when Romanticism predominates, a period whose borders are commonly confined to the nineteenth century, with some extension before and after. (Nor, it should be noted, is this book a history of nineteenth-

2 An English painter's view of a wild, sublime Romantic landscape. John Martin's *Manfred on the Jungfrau* (1837).

century music in all its aspects.) It is possible to sense the ground for this predominant Romanticism being prepared from the time in the 1740s when 'feeling' came to be consciously valued alongside if not in place of 'reason', and when the *galant* style was at its height. That intense aspect of the *galant* associated with the German term *Empfindsamkeit* (sentimentality, sensitivity), and exemplified in certain works of C. P. E. Bach, provided one notable anticipation, even though it occurred before Classicism itself had produced its own greatest achievements. Another precedent for Romanticism is found in the musical connections with the literary movement known as *Sturm und Drang* (storm and stress), after F. M. Klinger's play of that title of 1776, about the American Revolution, and which included plays by Goethe (*Götz von Berlichingen*, 1773) and Schiller (*Die Räuber*, 1780–81) among its more notable products. Musical manifestations of *Sturm und Drang* can be traced in the dramatic works of Gluck and others from the early 1760s, in Haydn's symphonies of

11

the early 1770s, like the *Trauersymphonie* and the *Farewell*, and they persist as late as Mozart's *Idomeneo* (1781). As with *Empfindsamkeit*, however, there was no simple progression from *Sturm und Drang* to Romanticism. Rather, the separation of the two reinforces the need to identify those quite different anticipations of Romantic expression within the Classical masters themselves: notably, of course, the later Mozart and the earlier Beethoven.

It will occasionally be argued today that Classicism and Romanticism are not just complementary, but represent qualities which have co-existed, in differing proportions, throughout the periods of musical history normally assigned to one or the other. This view has the advantage of reflecting feelings evident during the Romantic period itself – Schumann's, for example. Yet from a twentieth-century perspective it might well seem both futile and absurd to argue that what links Haydn and Wagner, or Mozart and Hugo Wolf, is more significant than what separates them; or that the change from Classic to Romantic is, in essence, a change of emphasis, not a sudden, total transformation of something into its polar opposite. It is undoubtedly a change with far-reaching consequences, decisively transforming the status and attitudes of the composer as well as his techniques. In purely musical respects, certain genres and forms are common to both Classicism and Romanticism, and there was a continued commitment to the Classically-based fundamentals of tonality and metrical periodicity throughout the Romantic era. Yet, even allowing for the large amount of overlap and interaction, such common features strengthen the sense of very profound differences, aesthetic and technical, reflecting different social circumstances, intellectual attitudes, and changing instrumental and practical resources. Romanticism may in essence be a matter of giving increasing emphasis to elements already present in Classicism. But those emphases – centring, it will be argued, most fundamentally on an increasing polarity between the search for the ideally organic and the willing embrace of the episodic, prompted in most cases by a desire to make music 'speak', programmatically – are as much a critique of Classicism as a tribute to it. The Romantic period, age or era grew out of, and vigorously away from, Classicism; and so powerful was that growth that when the twentieth century is too far in the past to be described as 'Modern', it may well be called the post-Romantic age.

One final introductory topic concerns the difficulty of defining those consequences or alternatives which retain Romantic characteristics: Nationalism, Realism, Impressionism, Expressionism. In all cases, it is necessary to identify a set of elements – matters of technique and style, language and usage – which justify such differentiations. The capacity for Nationalist, Impressionist or Expressionist features to co-exist with Romantic elements can certainly be demonstrated, although the relative radicalism of Impressionism may well lead to its most significant products, notably the mature works of Debussy, seeming distinctly detached from the more robust aspects of contemporary late Romanticism and Expressionism. With all such music, the challenge for the historian is to determine to what extent that which is non-Romantic is actually *anti*-Romantic. The same issue arises with Realism. Historians of literature and the visual arts are in no doubt that a distinctly anti-Romantic movement called Realism emerged in mid-century – an early example in painting would be Courbet's *A Burial at Ornans* (1849); in literature, Flaubert's *Madame Bovary* (1856). And while there is of course no difficulty in claiming that the subjects of certain operas – *La traviata*, *Carmen*, *Boris Godunov*, *La Bohème* – are more realistic, closer to (low) life or to the true history of a people, than others, it really needs to be shown that composers were using non-Romantic compositional techniques to achieve their Realist aims, if the term is to be suitable for application to music. This difficult matter will be touched on in later chapters, but it is worth making the general point here that the language of music remained basically Romantic throughout the century; indeed, as Carl Dahlhaus has argued, it was a case of music becoming in a sense anachronistic, of remaining Romantic in an age of Realism and Positivism.

Strictly speaking, no doubt, musical Romanticism is more style than language. It remained faithful, as indicated above, to tonality and to metrical periodicity: even its 'new' forms – symphonic poem, song cycle, music drama – were scarcely the result of a wholesale rejection of Classical precedents. Yet the radical differences in style between Schumann and Haydn, Wagner and Mozart, Brahms and Beethoven, do represent more than matters of mere surface, of emotion becoming more urgent and intense as form became freer and tone colour richer. Romantic music remained tonal, but it became more chromatic, more willing to give priority to melodic structural processes; it remained periodic, but phrase structure became less consistently regular; symphonies, sonatas and string quartets continued to be composed, but the emphasis was increasingly illustrative, the stimulus (however vaguely) increasingly extra-musical. These were the distinctive features of musical Romanticism, and it is perhaps the ultimate indication of that music's tendency to feel rather than think – at least initially – that it should so often seem, to the rational, inquiring mind, confused about its own status: not simply swayed by the dangerous ambition to enable speech to become music (to paraphrase Musorgsky), but uncertain how far its priorities could convincingly be more poetic than abstract, more organic than mosaic, more melodic than harmonic in origin. It may even be acceptable to claim that such 'confusion', which the greatest composers turned to such positive advantage, was the direct and close reflection of all those conflicts and confusions on the wider historical scene: of wars, social and political upheavals, of tensions between absolutism and democracy, imperial self-aggrandizement and national self-assertion, of disconcertingly rapid and radical advances in science and technology, and of far-reaching developments in

3 The uprising of March 1848, Milan. Of all 19th-century social and political upheavals, those of 1848 were notable for the involvement of artists and intellectuals. In Austrian-occupied Italy, Verdi's music was symbolic of national identity, yet in 1848 the composer was living in France (see Chapter 8).

philosophy and psychology, whose cultural consequences, however difficult to prove concretely, could scarcely be evaded by even the most determinedly other-worldly composer.

Romantic music undoubtedly reflects the particular instability of the era between the French and Russian revolutions, and shares, however indirectly, the uncertainties of that era about the nature of the truly just society, and of the place of minorities, élites and other potential sources of disturbance within that society. Yet this volume is necessarily a concise history of Romantic music, not a discussion in depth of that music in the perspective of history in general, and the term Romantic – with upper- or lower-case 'r' (in this text upper-case will be used except in quotations) – is as much a repository of allusion, an excuse for necessary imprecision, as the bearer of an unambiguous set of technical and aesthetic correlatives. It is nevertheless as inescapable today as it was in 1837 when Schumann declared: 'I am sick and tired of the word "romantic", though I have not spoken it ten times in my entire life. And yet, if I were to call our young seer [Stephen Heller] anything, it would be that.' Schumann was careful to avoid saying what exactly 'that' meant, and musical Romanticism is probably still best defined indirectly, through description and interpretation of particular compositions. There is a rich variety of masterpieces to serve the purpose, and to confirm that, whatever it is that makes Romantic music Romantic, the Romantic era was a time with a greatness all its own.

CHAPTER TWO

Shadow and stimulus:
the move away from Classicism

It is a good deal easier to proclaim that the *galant* and Classical masters were not primarily Romantics than it is to distinguish what is Romantic in their music from what is not. There are nevertheless certain unmistakable signs of features too disruptive, or too imprecise, to be suitable for full exploitation within Classicism itself. Reference has already been made to the *empfindsamer Stil* of C. P. E. Bach's fantasias and sonatas for keyboard, and to Haydn's symphonic *Sturm und Drang*. There is also an undeniable continuity between the often remarkably progressive and powerfully expressive dramatic manner of late Baroque and early Classical accompanied recitative and the tendency towards more continuous lyric melody of much Romantic opera. Perhaps the most striking feeling of proto-Romantic upheaval comes in the stormier passages of Gluck – like the finale of the ballet *Don Juan* (1761) – and, later, in the more overtly melancholy or turbulent movements by Mozart. There is of course abundant turbulence in Mozart's 'Don Juan' – the opera *Don Giovanni* (1787) – although his symphonic works in minor keys are models of an inextricable fusion of deep feeling and Classically controlled poise.

Beethoven's description of his piano sonatas op. 27 as 'Quasi una fantasia' may, with hindsight, be interpreted as the most transparent Classical declaration of anti-Classical intent, a conscious challenge to the aesthetic priorities of the Age of Reason. Beethoven's evident desire to try out new formal schemes and modes of expression in these two sonatas, composed in 1800–01, was an important step on the road to his visionary later masterpieces – especially the Diabelli Variations and the last five string quartets – which struck such awe into his successors, not least because they embody so enigmatic an interaction between two opposing tendencies: powerfully integrated, large-scale symphonic structures, and intense, self-contained miniatures in which the desire for authentic, individual expression seems to override the need to contribute obediently to a larger whole. Such vital foreshadowings of Romanticism were not the exclusive preserve of Germany and Austria, of course. Paris was an important musical centre and, as will soon become apparent, French music of the revolutionary period had a direct and fundamental role in the generation and development of Romanticism in Europe as a whole. Nevertheless, this narrative will begin with the Austro-German composers closest in time and place to the Classical masters, and in whom the evidence of movement away from the purest Classical principles is most apparent – Carl Maria von Weber (1786–1826) and Franz Schubert (1797–1828).

In both composers there is a fundamental change of emphasis, however strongly they may in some respects continue to reflect a commitment to the 'traditions' of the immediate past. For example, a song from Schubert's *Die schöne Müllerin* (1823) – *Die liebe Farbe* – is a fine instance of that restrained yet profound melancholy, introspective yet universal, which is an archetypal early Romantic quality. Classical melancholy has a stronger 'specific gravity': for example, in Pamina's aria 'Ach, ich fühl's' from *Die Zauberflöte* there is certainly more gravity, even a touch of Gluckian formality which, as in Gluck himself at his best, focuses the intensity of the expression rather than draining it away. With Schubert's greater musical simplicity goes greater potential instability – in the alternation of major and minor harmony, in the alternation of four- and five-bar phrases. Yet mood and method alike are precise and clearly outlined. While in all senses less 'substantial' than the Mozart aria, *Die liebe Farbe* is no less compelling a representation of a living mood.

For the complementary state of mind, we might instance the serenity of Agathe's aria 'Leise, leise' from Weber's *Der Freischütz*. Compared with the finest examples of Classical serenity – the slow movements of Mozart's concerto and quintet for clarinet, for example – there is again a sense of lesser substance, a relative lightness, touching and completely satisfying in its own terms, but something indicating the early stages of an artistic movement rather than the highest achievements of its richest phase. Weber's greatness is to make us forget such sober historical calculations so frequently. Yet it is perhaps when both Weber and Schubert explore more turbulent, disturbed emotions – the Wolf's Glen scene from *Freischütz*, the Heine setting *Der Atlas* – that the strengths of the new forms of expression are most obviously apparent. Of course, the game of

17

4 The Wolf's Glen scene from Weber's *Der Freischütz*, as staged in London in 1850. The setting shows a keen appreciation of the elements of Romantic landscape.

comparison can still place them at a disadvantage, as calling to mind any of the more titanic episodes from Beethoven's works will suggest. The fact remains that these and other examples of emotions in turmoil in early Romantic music offer the clearest indications of where the most exciting and far-reaching developments would take place in the later, wholly Romantic masters, while remaining supremely powerful and absorbing musical experiences in their own right.

In December 1824 Weber's *Der Freischütz* was performed (as *Robin des Bois*) in Paris: 'Not the real thing, but a gross travesty, hacked and mutilated in the most wanton fashion by an arranger.' The comment is that of Berlioz, who declared that 'even in this ravaged form there was a wild sweetness in the music that I found intoxicating'. This tribute from one Romantic to another is expressed in appropriately Romantic terms, down to the inclusion of one of Dr Johnson's adjectives – 'wild'. And it ties in neatly with the memory of another great Romantic. Wagner recalled his mother introducing him to Weber at the age of nine in 1822 with the memorable diagnosis that 'while I was wild about *Der Freischütz*, she had nevertheless noticed nothing in me that might suggest a talent for music'. Wagner's belief in his own talent also led him to write at length elsewhere about Weber's 'serious error', that 'pious faith in the omnipotence of pure melody', which prevented him from furthering the development of true music drama as determinedly as Wagner himself was eventually able to do.

It is often the case that composers who are regarded by critics of their own time as dangerously radical will be viewed by those of later generations as insufficiently adventurous. In Weber's case, even his fellow composers seem to have conformed to critical convention. Schubert preferred *Der Freischütz* (1821) to the later, more advanced *Euryanthe* (1823), complaining of the latter that whenever a scrap of tune appears, it is crushed like a mouse in a trap by the weighty orchestration'. For Wagner, thirty years after Schubert, the problem with *Euryanthe* was too much tune rather than too little, and the work is a 'true and beautiful success only where, for love of truth, he quite renounces absolute melody, and – as in the opening scene of the first act – gives the noblest, most faithful musical expression to the emotional dramatic declamation as such'.

Such differences of opinion are the natural result of changes of historical perspective, but they help to ensure that the evaluation of the nature and extent of Weber's Romanticism remains a particularly delicate matter. Since he was born in 1786, sixteen years after Beethoven and eleven years before Schubert (and died in 1826, before either of them), his music might be expected to contain more evidence of Classical traits than Schubert's. That this is not the case may have much to do with the fact that Weber (born in north Germany) was never based in Vienna, and was therefore in more direct contact with progressive German thinking. That progressive-ness was born to a large degree of frustrated nationalism: of dissatisfaction both with Prussian domination in Germany and with the absence of unity represented by the multitude of separate states – about three hundred of them – which made Germany such a relatively easy target for Napoleon. Progressiveness in the arts may not always reject an element of escapism, and it can certainly be argued that the enthusiasm of the young German Romantics – philosophers and poets as well as musicians – for the great legends of the past, and the folk art of the present, potentially provided a less than adequate response to the need for new, positive cultural forces to counter decadence and disunity. Yet the new forces were so strong precisely because they arose as much by instinct as by intellectual contrivance, and in Weber's case all circumstances seemed to conspire to equip him for a role of central significance. If, as is frequently stated by historians, Romanticism owed much of its impetus to a reaction of the rural against the urban, expressed by particular sensitivity to the inexplicable, even superhuman factors evident in the natural world, and by the propensity for sensing the artistic potential of the iconoclastic, as opposed to the orderly and conformist, then Weber's Romantic pedigree was impeccable. Even so, he was never able to indulge the luxury of retiring from city life to commune with nature and create anti-Enlightenment art from the security of an Ivory Tower built and sustained on personal wealth. Weber was a hardworking practical musician who became, pre-eminently, a man of the theatre – so much so that he can be claimed as the German who brought Romanticism successfully into the theatre, dramatists like Tieck and Schlegel having failed. Weber was also fortunate in being taught by an important (if, today, little regarded) *Sturm und Drang* composer, G. J. Vogler – who taught Meyerbeer; and there were also crucial contacts with progressive thinkers like Schelling. Weber's first complete three-act stage work, *Silvana* (1808–10), was originally described as a 'Romantic Opera', and although it may be impossible to establish what the composer himself meant by the term, it is known that he was studying Schelling at the time of its composition. Schelling's philosophical writings had a strong appeal for many Romantic artists, and Weber had become familiar with his work before settling in Dresden, where he spent the longest part of his working life – 1817–26 – and where the principal literary influences were Tieck, Schlegel and Wackenroder. It therefore seems certain that Schelling, whom Weber had got to know personally in Munich in 1811, after *Silvana* but well before *Der Freischütz*, had a strong influence on the development of the composer's views about how a new emphasis in musical drama might come about. Above all, it was

Schelling's bringing together of man and nature, spirit and nature, to find their ideal fusion in art – in strong contrast to the Classical tendency to keep man and nature (rational being and instinctive force) distinct – that stimulated the poetic imagination, and programmatic techniques, of early Romantic music. And for Weber it was the theatre, and opera, which provided the most natural and effective outlet for these ideas.

There was nevertheless more to German musical Romanticism than an attraction to philosophy and the theatre. As already suggested, the revolt of country against town helped to promote a sympathy for folksong and folktale: a fruitful source for the constant and highly productive tensions between simple folklike materials and sophisticated forms and technical processes found in much later nineteenth-century music. For Weber, in any case, it was nature, rather than any specific manifestations of folk art, which provided the strongest stimulus, as revealed in his startling statement: 'The contemplation of a landscape is to me the performance of a piece of music'. Yet no great composer is likely to progress very far by means of extra-musical stimuli alone, and it should be stressed that if Weber's greatest single achievement was the creation of German Romantic opera, then he found his most powerful inspiration for this enterprise not in Germany but in France.

The origins of French musical Romanticism will be explored in Chapter Five. Here it is sufficient to note that a line from Rousseau and the likes of Grétry, Dalayrac, Berton, Gaveaux, Cherubini, Méhul and Boieldieu, provides the most convincing path to *Der Freischütz*: moreover, a glance at the repertory performed by Weber during his years in Prague (1813–15) confirms his familiarity with the French *opéra comique*. It is not even that *Der Freischütz* is incontrovertibly the very first German Romantic opera: that honour could well be accorded to Spohr's *Faust* (1813), first performed in 1816, the year before *Der Freischütz* was begun. Spohr's reliance on French models in *Faust* is much more evident than Weber's in *Der Freischütz*. And so, while French sources can be identified in the latter – for example, Weber's Aennchen is close to the soubrette of *opéra comique*; Max's music calls Méhul to mind; and the melodrama of the Wolf's Glen scene and the use of thematic reminiscence are both more French than German – yet there is no sense of slavish reliance on a different tradition. Indeed, the more one recognizes the connections between *Der Freischütz* and other, earlier operas of any country, the more impressive Weber's ability to advance beyond imitation into imaginative transformation appears. And it is undoubtedly the case that such a wealth of sources and precedents makes the actual freshness and dramatic vitality of *Der Freischütz* the more remarkable. Even its flaws add to its charm, simply because the flaws are much more in the plot than in the music.

If one measure of Weber's importance was his ability to absorb such a diversity of influences and make the result so personal, another measure was his ability to advance from that base to a work – *Euryanthe* – that is a good deal more original and independent of precedents, French or otherwise. With *Euryanthe* it is much more a case of the significance of its influence on later music than of the opera having any major antecedents of its own – though Méhul's *Ariodant* (1799) has been offered as one possible source. Moreover, remembering comments like those of Schubert and Wagner quoted above (p. 19), it is tempting to discuss *Euryanthe* solely in terms of its progressiveness: of the *Lohengrin*-like music at the end of Act II scene 1, or a passage like the villainess Eglantine's outburst in Act III (no. 23), where guilt drives her to the edge of madness, and Weber depicts her fraught state with powerful economy – a brief, explosive motive in the orchestra and harmony that becomes increasingly unstable. There are certainly places where Weber's zeal for the realistic emotion which throughcomposed arioso can unleash leads him to risk harmony that is not so much unstable as structurally undefined. But there are things in *Euryanthe* which echo down through German opera at least as far as *Siegfried* – compare the turbulent depiction of Adolar's fight with the serpent (Act III, no. 16) with the stormy music at the beginning of Act III of Wagner's drama. Weber is undoubtedly supreme in *Euryanthe*, as in *Freischütz*, in the representation of both rage (Lysiart's Act II aria, no. 10) and repose (Euryanthe's two cavatinas – 'Glöcklein im Tale' and 'Hier dicht am Quell'). Attempts to express the more heroic, decisive side of Euryanthe herself are, perhaps understandably, less successful: when in Act III she exhorts the King and his huntsmen to lead her back to her beloved Adolar the rhythms become four-square, the orchestral accompaniment musically basic rather than dramatically responsive: but even Wagner took some time to master comparable situations, as the relative feebleness of the end of Act I of *Tannhäuser* graphically illustrates. Perhaps the most remarkable thing about *Euryanthe* is not its progressive harmony, or use of thematic reminiscence, but its formal and expressive flexibility, and its essential, affecting simplicity. At the very end, the brief, and dramatically distinctly inept duet of reunion and reconciliation for Euryanthe and Adolar is separated from the final (equally brief) chorus of acclamation by a short, almost purely diatonic passage of gentle arioso in which Adolar provides a final, necessary piece of narration. Weber's concern here is less with smooth transition than with dramatic effect. And however awkward the drama itself, it works, musically, supremely well.

Euryanthe is generally regarded as superior to Weber's last opera, *Oberon* (1826), written for London, in which spoken dialogue

5 Portrait of Weber by John Cawse, painted between March and June 1826, when Weber was in London preparing the première of *Oberon*. He died, aged 39, on 5 June 1826.

reappears. Nevertheless, *Oberon* is still one of the finest operas of its time, and it brings together elements from all Weber's earlier stage works to produce a synthesis none the less masterly for being the last work of a composer who, had he lived, could scarcely have failed to reach still greater heights. *Oberon* confirms the essential and resourceful Romanticism of Weber's last decade; and it also underlines those progressive features of operatic design – the tendency to more continuous and flexible forms, the presence of leitmotif, the beautifully orchestrated evocations of nature, and the significant interaction of human characters with the natural world – which make Weber so potent a precursor of Wagner.

Weber's involvement with the theatre was not simply that of conductor and composer. In Dresden, as Royal Saxon Kapellmeister, he was responsible for every aspect of planning and production, and this represents the practical result of his belief in a principle which, under the title *Gesamtkunstwerk*, has been used so widely – and often unwisely – to describe later aspirations. Dresden itself was far from a forward-looking powerhouse of new ideas and enterprises, and it may well be true that there was an element of quixotic – and Romantic – masochism in Weber's unwillingness to seek more congenial surroundings – a feeling that only through suffering would anything worthwhile be achieved. Whether this is true or not, it is undeniable that Weber, even if not the most versatile of composers, became the first all-round master of musical Romanticism, through composition, administration and literary work as well as through his role in various clubs and societies like Dresden's Harmonischer Verein. As suggested earlier, however infrequently the word 'Romantic' may have been used in the deliberations of such bodies, it cannot be doubted that, in their concern with contemporary developments and the new ideas in aesthetics and literary criticism, they were aware of the issues central to what we now call Romanticism, and to a greater extent than would appear to have been the case in contemporary Vienna.

As often with close contemporaries, comparison of Weber and Schubert naturally tends towards an emphasis on the complementary nature of their achievements: Weber pre-eminent in opera but uninterested in the Lied, an indifferent symphonist and an early exponent of the new pianistic virtuosity which would find fulfilment in the 1830s in Chopin and Liszt; Schubert indifferent in opera yet supreme in Lieder, pre-eminent in symphonic works of all kinds, and using the piano in ways which have little to do with display as Chopin or Liszt conceived it. One consequence of such summary comparisons is that it can become difficult for historians to identify all aspects of Schubert's greatness as having to do with Romanticism: and his was perhaps a richer, more complex achievement than Weber's in that what *is* Romantic is often intriguingly framed by, even fused with, Classical qualities. It is not just because of his residence in Vienna that Schubert seems much closer to Beethoven than Weber does.

Schubert's failings as an opera composer are usually offered as an exemplary demonstration of composers needing to recognize where they belong. There is clearly the greatest contrast between the lively intimacy of the domestic Schubertiade, where the composer's Romanticism could find its most natural and original expression, and the public arena of the opera house in Vienna which, after 1817, was dominated by Rossini. The point is not that Rossini was the purest Classicist, a latterday Mozart – he had his own Romantic qualities – but that Schubert was no more successful at adapting a song style to opera (*Alfonso ed Estrella*, 1821–2) than he was in imitating the favoured Italian or French operatic models (*Fierrabras*, 1823). The great masters of the Lied, at least before Richard Strauss, were not, on the whole, successful in the opera house, and we should be grateful that, in Schubert's case, his supreme fertility ensured that the energies expended in opera composition did not prevent him from composing so many great songs.

To acclaim the setting which Schubert made in October 1814 of the poem from Goethe's *Faust* called *Gretchen am Spinnrade* is to locate with some precision the first memorable musical portrayal of one of the great themes of Romantic song, the restless dissatisfaction with life in general and love in particular. What *Gretchen*, and all Schubert's greatest songs, do is narrow the dramatic focus so that the reflections of an individual (any kind of individual, from Prometheus or Atlas to the anti-heroic protagonists of *Die schöne Müllerin* and *Die Winterreise*) are conveyed with the greatest concentration and intensity. The art of the art song is to achieve direct emotional communication by means of allusion and symbolism, without mimetic gesture or scenery. The Lieder singer is not an impersonator like the operatic actor: and so the music, in form and content, must embody its subject-matter with the greatest naturalness and power if the song is not to seem too obviously a work of art about expression rather than expression itself. After all, it will be performed in an atmosphere very different from that of the opera house, and demands a very different kind of attitude from its audience.

Schubert's work as a teacher, and his friendships with poets and painters (minor, for the most part), are generally held to indicate his importance in relation to the new willingness of the increasingly powerful, relatively well-educated middle class to take an interest in the arts. Yet, as the cramped conditions and rather self-satisfied expressions of the famous drawing (*c*.1860) by Schubert's friend Moritz von Schwind suggest, such interest might well tend most naturally to promote a deadening mediocrity, if not an anti-Romantic revolt of urban against rural. Historians have not been slow to stress Schubert's evident bourgeois or Biedermeier traits, or to

6 Moritz von Schwind's recollection of a Schubert evening at Joseph von Spaun's. The composer is at the piano, with the baritone Johann Michael Vogl on his right.

ponder the irony inherent in the fact that his willingness to write songs purely to please his own circle of friends could result in music of very unBiedermeier-like force and passion. And it is with such force and passion that Romanticism asserts itself. What matters with Schubert, then, is not so much the society in which he lived, and the stimuli or provocations it provided, as the deep, inbuilt blend of technical resource and expressive clarity and veracity which enabled him to respond to those stimuli with great music. More than Weber, it seems, he became a Romantic despite his environment, and even a cosy fireside song like *Der Einsame* is so pointedly turned in musical terms as to be very far from the kind of portentous celebration of domestic virtues in which, for example, so much nineteenth-century English song was to indulge. More importantly, in some of Schubert's most sublime music the simplest, most mundane elements of dance or song are magically enhanced, not by being transformed out of all recognition but by his sheer green-fingered sensitivity to their essence and their potential. As a single example of this magic, I would instance *Das Fischermädchen* from *Schwanengesang*, which achieves greatness not just through the freshness of its melody and the attractive lilt of its rhythms, but through the way in which the ambiguities of Heine's text promote subtle irregularities of phrase structure and unexpected enrichments of harmony.

Another property of genius is the ability to sense things 'in the air' – the kind of generally circulating ideas and procedures which can easily lead historians and critics to unguarded assumptions about 'influence'. Sometimes musicology can essay a plausible answer to the question of whether such connections are the result of direct and conscious borrowing, or simply the outcome of creative minds thinking alike; and analysis can strengthen a conviction about the former by showing the links between model and modification. To take a celebrated example: the alternation of major and minor harmony noted earlier in *Die liebe Farbe* has clear precedents in French music. Yet it is scarcely surprising that this particular device is more closely associated with Schubert than, say, with Méhul; a song like *Die liebe Farbe* burns itself into the consciousness in a way nothing by Méhul – important historical figure though he undoubtedly is – has done or is ever likely to do. In other words, by far the most interesting 'influences' are those connecting one major master with another: and it is precisely the desire to escape this kind of influence that is likely to motivate a major master when he listens to his contemporaries and predecessors.

Die liebe Farbe, described in general terms on p. 17 above, is the simplest type of Lied: strophic (i.e. each stanza set to the same music), almost entirely syllabic, its short piano prelude also doing duty as postlude. It is a song about repetition, and Müller's use of rhyme, not just at the ends of lines, but between adjacent words – 'ich'/'mich', 'Schatz'/'hat's' – as well as the repetitions of 'grün' itself, may have prompted the composer's tolling dominant pedal: that, and the associations with funereal bells. The melody has the kind of shapely poise which might, in lesser hands, lapse into an effete refinement, a draining of active emotion. What restores and shores up real feeling is the harmony: the major–minor alternations are so telling that no richer chromaticism or complexities are needed to ensure its effect.

This is the essence of Romanticism in miniature. As the Lied developed, in Schubert himself as much as in later composers, it became increasingly important that the piano 'accompaniment' contributed as fully as possible to the creation of atmosphere, and to the portrayal of those expressive essences which might be felt to underpin the 'mere' words of the poem. Even in *Die liebe Farbe* the accompaniment, though relatively modest in scope, is so eminently symbolic that the text itself seems to become a gloss on what is most essential to the song's expressive character, rather than the prime source of that expression. Nevertheless, the appreciation of the Romantic Lied from Schubert to Richard Strauss depends not on forgetting the text but on remembering it through the music. In this sense, the dimensions of the text itself are never exceeded, even in songs as 'symphonic' as Wolf's Goethe settings *Prometheus* or *Grenzen der Menschheit*. Indeed, the notion of 'symphonic' here is so loose as to be unnecessary to a full appreciation of the dramatic force of what are, in essence, large-scale songs and nothing more, even with the orchestral versions of their accompaniments.

The idea of loosening the notion of what is symphonic is often proposed as essential to true Romanticism. The symphony strides towards its Mahlerian fulfilment of Beethoven's ideal, the argument runs: not only are the millions embraced, in obedience to Schiller's instructions, but the whole world is drawn into the frame. As a late Classic, early Romantic composer of symphonic music, Schubert's role in this process is crucial, yet open to notably different interpretations. Schumann, whose dislike of the term 'Romantic' has been quoted in Chapter One, was in no doubt that – in the field of the piano sonata, at least – 'Beethoven's example was followed mainly by Franz Schubert, who sought after new terrain and won it'. Moreover, one reason for the greatness of the *Great* C major Symphony was that 'over the whole there is poured out that romanticism we know to be characteristic of Franz Schubert'. Today, Schubert continues to fascinate precisely because the relation between the old terrain and the new is so tantalizingly ambiguous, and nowhere are these differences more extreme than in reactions to his symphonic music. All commentators will agree that Schubert was unable to dispense entirely with Classical forms, even had he wished to do so: where disagreement arises is in determining the nature and significance – the Romanticism – of his modifications to – even distortions of – those forms.

Undoubtedly the most personal Schubertian trait in instrumental music is expansion: not just the introduction of longer, more lyrical themes than one finds in Beethoven's large-scale movements, but the use of richer, less diatonic tonal relations – as in his last and finest Piano Sonata, in B flat, in which the relatively leisurely nature of the outer movements contrasts sharply with Beethoven's most typical concentration and dynamism. And even in those other late works which seem closer to Classical precedents – the G major String Quartet, the C major Quintet, the *Great* C major Symphony – there is an expansiveness which, while not demonstrating an irreversible shift from harmonic to thematic principles of structuring, or from forms based on the expansion of a unity to forms composed of the balancing of contrasts, does confirm Schubert's ability to admit a high degree of lyric reflection into sonata movements without simply breaking up the form into a succession of juxtaposed episodes. An earlier work, the superb A minor String Quartet (1824), demonstrates that he was perfectly capable of greater concentration and economy, with no loss of lyric poignancy and melodic eloquence. No one is likely to mistake this work for imitation Beethoven; indeed, it is more as if Schubert is seeking to explore the relevance of forms in which Beethoven was uniquely at home to his own very different musical temperament.

Recently, specialist studies have tended to focus less on awkward comparisons between Schubert and his contemporaries and more on the fruitful consequences of his innovations, whether in the multi-movement sonata works of Bruckner and Brahms, or in compositions (from Liszt to Schoenberg and beyond) which link separate movements together after the fashion of the *Wanderer* Fantasia and the F minor Fantasy for piano duet. What keeps these large-scale symphonic works of Schubert's in the public eye is the often supreme beauty of their melodic materials and the compelling way in which those melodies are harmonically enriched. In loosening the unifying grip of Classical formal schemes, these enrichments and expansions simply acknowledge the need of their materials, not to flaunt themselves rhapsodically with no particular end in view, but for room in which to breathe and to realize their full potential within larger schemes whose allegiance is still, essentially, to Classic tradition. It is one of the essential qualities of the Romantic era that melodies have as much right to exist in symphonic music as motifs have in dramatic music. As a result, there grows a rich confusion of genres, and an eager appreciation by composers themselves of the fact that coherence can survive the loss of the stricter unifying schemes so powerfully evident in Classical times. For his role in furthering this confusion, this appreciation, Schubert can certainly not be excluded from any account of musical Romanticism. Still less can he be excluded when the other, complementary aspect of his genius is recalled. Some of his greatest songs are his shortest: there is a place for concentration as well as expansion in the world of Romanticism, and Schubert was a master of both.

CHAPTER THREE

'A gracious, well-bred air':
Romanticism in Germany before Wagner

The deaths of Weber and Schubert, as well as Beethoven, within two and a half years, between June 1826 and November 1828, might well seem to mark the end of the period of overlap between Classical and Romantic forms of expression. There was nevertheless one other important composer whose long life linked the age of Mozart to the age of Wagner. Louis Spohr was born in 1784, two years before the composition of *Figaro*, and died in 1859, the year of *Tristan*'s completion. Moreover, in 1808, even before Hoffmann's essay on Beethoven, a reviewer commented that Spohr's 'compositions as a whole have, more or less, a character of spirited yet temperate seriousness and an agreeable mixture of gloomy and tender melancholy. If one should call this Romantic the present critic would not object'. That same year, Spohr composed a 'grand Romantic opera' in three acts, *Alruna die Eulenkönigin* (*Alruna, the Queen of the Owls*). But it was his *Faust* (composed in 1813, first performed in 1816, with revisions in 1818 and 1852) which placed Spohr in the forefront of progressive Romanticism, not least because its use of leitmotif is as thoroughgoing as any before Wagner's. In *Faust* it is possible to distinguish between thematic reminiscences, ideas which recur without significant change, and leitmotifs, relatively brief melodic phrases representing such potent dramatic forces as 'love' and 'hell', which are used in ways which vary considerably according to musical context.

Yet for all his progressiveness Spohr made less impact than Weber, even in his lifetime, and (as argued in Chapter Two) it is *Der Freischütz*, with its directness and its sense of capturing the spirit of the times, which is rightly seen as the true originator of German musical Romanticism. Spohr, it seems, failed to rouse his audiences to comparable fervour. This verdict was confirmed by no less a critic than Hugo Wolf, writing in 1884, and reflecting the common view of that time that 'Romanticism' was already in the past: 'In accordance with the trend of the time, he [Spohr] was a romanticist, and if one

31

misses in his operas the fresh, robust folk character of Weber's muse, then the fault may lie in his soft nature, which commuted the fiery pulse of human sensibility to his musical powers of expression not directly, but diluted, as reflected in a somewhat sickly sentimentality'. Spohr embodied the paradox of the pioneer – for example, his E minor Violin Concerto of 1814 has an unmistakably and, for its time, quite exceptionally Romantic atmosphere. Yet that relative lack of punch and passion which may have been 'progressive' in the age of Beethoven inevitably seemed passé in the age of the young Wagner. Spohr was in many respects an attractive character, far from timid in his dealings with patrons, and willing and able, at the age of sixty-four, to help man the barricades in Kassel during the 1848 upheavals: comparisons with Wagner in Dresden should be noted. His candid responses to music more radical than his own also provide revealing insights into the (intelligent) attitudes of the time: for example, at the time of his performances in Kassel of *Der fliegende Holländer* in 1843, Spohr wrote of the work as 'approaching the new Romantic music à la Berlioz'. He considered Wagner 'the most gifted of all our dramatic composers of the present time', and his later reservations about *Tannhäuser* – 'much that at first was very disagreeable to me I have become accustomed to with frequent hearings; only the lack of rhythm and the frequent absence of rounded periods is still very objectionable to me' – pinpoint those aspects of Wagner's work which were to develop into the new music drama. But Berlioz's report of the French verdict on *Jessonda* (1823) – 'dull, without character, lacking in élan, in contrasts, in variety, in fresh, grand or brilliant ideas, that which gives life to music and especially to dramatic music' (*Journal des Débats*, 30 April 1842) – while contrasting strongly with such eulogies as that of the English critic who, after Mendelssohn's death, proclaimed Spohr 'the first composer of the day, without a possible rival' (*Morning Chronicle*, 2 May 1848), indicates why his work has lasted less well than that of Mendelssohn himself, or Schumann. Spohr's Romanticism developed too early for enough fire and fantasy to survive into the 1830s and '40s, and the role of leader passed to others.

Felix Mendelssohn (1809–47) belongs to the generation after Spohr, Weber and Schubert. Yet by the middle of the 1820s he had already composed a great deal of music, including two of his most celebrated works, the Octet op. 20 (1825) and the Overture to *A Midsummer Night's Dream* op. 21 (1826). With these works, composed in Berlin, it could be claimed that symphonic music made the decisive advance from Classicism to Romanticism, as opera had done in the same decade with Weber. Certainly their tone is quite different from that of the (Viennese) late Beethoven and Schubert: and yet their very originality made them something of a false dawn – not least for Mendelssohn himself. Wolf's verdict on Spohr as a symphonist – 'he lacked just that universality characteristic of Mozart and Beethoven, the greatest geniuses of them all' – applies to Mendelssohn too, and his very originality was a handicap, to the extent that he evidently found it difficult to sustain its momentum, impossible to build further on its foundations in his later years. The ease with substantial forms and the evolutionary flow of fresh yet sharply characterized ideas which make the Octet and the Overture so memorable could, fortunately, be recaptured from time to time – most notably in the relatively late Violin Concerto (1844) and C minor Piano Trio (1845).

Nevertheless, the contemporary judgment of Mendelssohn, expressed most cogently by Robert Schumann (1810–56), is likely to seem overstated today. For Schumann, he was the Mozart rather than the Beethoven of the nineteenth century: 'The most brilliant musician, the one who sees most clearly through the contradictions of this period, and for the first time reconciles them'. But Schumann added: 'After Mozart came Beethoven; this new Mozart will also be followed by a Beethoven – perhaps he is already born'. And Schumann, while unfailingly appreciative of Mendelssohn's superiority to the vast majority of contemporary German composers, was skilful enough to make the necessary comparisons with Beethoven and Schubert in such a way as to avoid unduly exaggerating the achievements of his friend and colleague. Discussing Mendelssohn's Symphony no. 3 (*Scottish*, completed 1843) alongside Schubert's *Great* C major, Schumann remarks that 'the more recent of the two has a more gracious, well-bred air, and is the more readily accessible. But Schubert's symphony has other excellencies; it shows, particularly, a richer inventiveness'. And Schumann's highest praise was to rank Mendelssohn's achievement as equivalent to that of his great Classic predecessors: the D minor Trio (1839) 'is the master-trio of the present, just as in their times were the trios of Beethoven in B flat and D, and that of Schubert in E flat'.

Where Schumann might seem over-generous to Mendelssohn is in his claim that he 'sees most clearly through the contradictions of this period, and for the first time reconciles them'. Schumann does not state here what those 'contradictions' were, though we may suspect that they involved the need, as he saw it, to build on the formal foundations of the immediate (Classical) past while taking advantage of the new (Romantic) qualities of expression. It could indeed be argued that Mendelssohn's well-to-do background and thorough education seemed to prepare him to establish precisely such a synthesis of old and new, and he was able to follow up the Octet and *Midsummer Night's Dream* Overture with several works which reinforce their achievements: notably the op. 12 String Quartet (1829) and the *Hebrides* Overture (1830). Nevertheless, it seems at least arguable that instead of envisaging a synthesis of (in essence) Classical and Romantic qualities, Mendelssohn sensed conflict. His own musical predilections were for Bach, Handel and Mozart, and the more Romantic stimuli which impinged on him were literary, extra-musical. Yet it is an oversimplification to conclude that these characteristics make him more a latterday Classicist than a Romantic. As with most of his German contemporaries, his truly Romantic impulses were able to find expression in a series of poetic miniatures –

7 Contemporary engraving of Fingal's Cave, on the island of Staffa, Inner Hebrides. Mendelssohn's *Hebrides* Overture (1830) is a finely evocative piece of musical landscape painting.

the *Songs without Words* for piano – which are absolutely of their time, and have nothing in the least Neoclassical about them. Indeed, Mendelssohn is surely only a Neoclassicist (accepting that the term has none of the twentieth century's connotations of parodist or pasticheur) if that means a contrast in his work as a whole between compositions which strive to retain eighteenth-century forms and characteristics and those which do not.

Mendelssohn's failure to fulfil his exceptional early promise may be ascribed to purely musical causes, especially the fact that he emerged too soon: a longer period of assimilation was needed before music could advance confidently beyond Beethoven and Schubert. Yet, dangerous though the exercise may be, the question of his character and personality cannot be excluded from consideration. On the surface, his advantages were obvious. He was as well-educated and widely travelled as, for example, Berlioz: unlike Berlioz, he was successful in his own country, had a happy marriage and strong family support. A little knowledge of psychology might prompt the reflection that it was all too good to be true. It could be that too much was expected of the prodigy, by people well able to evaluate his achievement, and that, from fear of failure, Mendelssohn dissipated – or dammed – his energies; alternatively, he never matured

8 The Gewandhaus, Leipzig, in 1845. Mendelssohn was conductor of the orchestra there from 1835 to 1846, achieving notable advances in standards of performance and breadth of repertoire.

emotionally to a sufficient extent to sustain, still less to consolidate, his adolescent genius. Nevertheless, even if his greatest service to nineteenth-century music was as a conductor and administrator, notably in Leipzig from 1835 to 1846, his best compositions (from which not all music-lovers would exclude the *Scottish*, *Italian* and *Reformation* symphonies) are an ineradicable part of the Romantic century's formative (and perhaps purest) phase. Above all, Mendelssohn's life and work, his compositions and his other musical activities, bear witness to the separation in German musical life during his time between theatre and concert-hall or salon – between operatic and non-operatic music. And what is remarkable about this phase of musical Romanticism is that a composer like Mendelssohn could become a leading figure despite his inability to conquer the opera house.

Convenient though it is to consider the close contemporaries Schumann and Mendelssohn in terms of contrasts – to play off Mendelssohn's cosmopolitan experience and early success against Schumann's lack of foreign travel and much less spectacular growth to creative maturity – their shared inability to create masterpieces of dramatic music reveals something very fundamental about German music between Weber and Wagner. Yet the failures were very different in kind. Mendelssohn, despite a lifelong ambition to succeed in opera, is best known today as the skilful provider of incidental music for spoken drama; and it is on his oratorios *St Paul* (1834–6) and *Elijah* (1846) – especially the latter, with its many vivid and vigorous episodes – that any thought of him as a music dramatist will be concentrated. Schumann, although he completed only one stage work, *Genoveva* (1850), and that generally hailed as a disaster, was a very different case, whose failure, in terms of the evolution of Romantic music, is a good deal more significant. And the significance lies in one simple question: why was lasting success in opera (for a truly major German composer) so difficult after Weber – at least until Wagner began to make his presence felt?

Historians usually point to a combination of lack of will on the part of composers, and a corresponding lack of demand in society. Opera audiences in Germany were content to explore offerings from France and Italy, by Auber, Adam, Bellini or Donizetti, or German works inspired by these. Nevertheless, if Spohr's greater German contemporaries lacked the fierce, egotistic will-power that would eventually drive Wagner to revolutionize all aspects of operatic composition, performance and production, they were not lacking in the ambition and vision to develop very different but no less Romantic forms of expression, notably in solo piano music and the Lied.

Schumann's critical writings encourage us to read a clear, coherent theory of musical Romanticism into their committed and often caustic pages: and they also shed considerable light on Schumann's own priorities as a composer. He was highly sensitive to music's increasing historical perspective, as no one aware of Mendelssohn's celebrated revival of Bach could fail to be. And yet that perspective was very different from that considered orthodox today. Bach was important not so much for his powerful, purposeful mastery of form and techniques as for what Schumann felt to be qualities of spirit, of atmosphere, which Schumann's own contemporaries could respond to and reflect. The century between Bach and Schumann himself was therefore seen essentially in terms of progress towards the contemporary Romanticism: 'Mendelssohn, Bennett, Chopin, Hiller, all the so-called romantics (I mean the Germans, of course) are in their music much closer to Bach than Mozart was; all of them have a most thorough knowledge of Bach'.

Nevertheless, it was Beethoven, not Bach, who was seen as Romanticism's chief progenitor, and it was on Beethoven's foundation – already built on by the still little-known Schubert, as Schumann pointed out as early as 1835 – that 'there has arisen, whether consciously or unconsciously, a new school, not yet fully developed and recognized'. The 'new school' may have been able to identify the new freedoms won for it by Beethoven and Schubert and other pioneers such as John Field. But it proved understandably difficult for most composers to match the achievements of such pioneers, and even more difficult to build at all securely on their foundations. Schumann regarded the case of Chopin as especially significant – for here was a musician, by some way the most talented and individual of the pianist–composers based in Paris, who seemed content to exploit the style, and the (usually) miniature forms, developed early in his career. Chopin had failed to recognize his 'duty' to music in its post-Beethoven phase, and Schumann evidently felt that to appear to reject the principles of the Classical sonata tradition rather than to build on them was ultimately a betrayal. As

Chapter Six will argue, such an interpretation is scarcely fair to Chopin. But it gives a clear explanation of the motivation for Schumann's own later development, in which the year 1841 was the great turning point. With Clara's prompting, he sought ways of remaining true to his own Romantic canons of expression while giving due acknowledgment to thé larger forms and cooler disciplines of Classical tradition. Yet his quest for ways of absorbing the old into the new was, at best, only partly successful; and even those who go out of their way to seek and find virtues in Schumann's later symphonic music are likely to discover their admiration for what he achieved before 1841 strengthened by the experience.

The 1830s were, for Schumann, a decade of the piano, and one only has to select from his output some of the most celebrated titles – *Papillons* (1829–31), *Carnaval* (1833–5), *Symphonic Studies* (1834–7), *Davidsbündlertänze* (1837), *Phantasie* (1836–8), *Kreisleriana* (1838), *Kinderszenen* (1838) – to realize the substance, distinction and variety of his contribution to Romantic music. Here was a personal, poetic utterance, by no means always on the scale of a miniature, which was deeply involved with the literary, yet intensely satisfying in purely musical terms – original, yet accessible. It is tempting to take Schumann's literary bias, attach it to his evident post-Classical attitude – the preference for collections of short and relatively self-contained pieces rather than the larger, dynamically structured Classical forms – and then conclude that what is most precious in his work is the vividness of those single moods, the refinements of those self-contained pieces. Yet when Schumann himself claimed, of *Carnaval*, that 'the whole has no artistic value whatever: the manifold states of soul alone seem to me of interest', he was not, to say the least, telling the whole story. There is undoubtedly more to *Carnaval*, and to all Schumann's major piano cycles, than the simple succession of its parts. They offer a cumulative balancing of contrasts that is looser, freer than that of the Classical sonata: less concerned with an overriding unity, perhaps, but coherent as a whole and (with the possible exception of the *Symphonic Studies*) suffering if movements are omitted or re-ordered.

Even in the 1830s, Schumann wrote sonatas and attempted other symphonic works, though relatively ill at ease with formal principles and compositional techniques that had so little in common with his own most personal mode of expression. The C major *Phantasie* op. 17

is the great exception proving this rule – a large-scale, broadly conceived, three-movement structure which may merit the label 'symphonic' on account of its size and scope, yet is far from a typical sonata. As homage to Beethoven, it pays the master the supreme tribute of shunning imitation – if not quotation – and striking out boldly into a new world. For Charles Rosen, a fine interpreter of the piece, the *Phantasie* is a 'totally unclassical' work, a 'monument that commemorates the death of the classical style'. And Hugo Wolf, after a performance of the work by Anton Rubinstein in Vienna in 1884, wrote: 'I had the feeling that Schumann, in the first movement of his Fantasie, had struck the fundamental tone of the romanticists' character, that sorrow-suffused plaint of nature which, sounding through all the vicissitudes of life, finally expires in a melancholy vision of harmony with nature, and in the upward surging and softly subsiding broken chords, had let it fade away – a swansong of romanticism'. Today, the *Phantasie* will probably seem more 'a monument that commemorates the death of the classical style' than 'a swansong of romanticism'. But it is pre-eminently a monument to the way in which a great composer, within a decade of the deaths of Beethoven and Schubert, could imagine a new world.

That new world was strongly indebted to developments in 'piano technology', as the instrument itself continued to evolve into the modern concert grand, and public demand for displays of virtuosity remained buoyant. Schumann's own traumatic experiences as a would-be virtuoso are well known, although it is far from certain whether the finger problems which afflicted him in 1832 were the result of the notorious 'mechanical device' or of mercury poisoning, a consequence of treatment for syphilis. Schumann was not concerned to make his own piano music easy to play, and yet his evident and consistent contempt for the shallow pyrotechnics of those executants based mainly in Paris – Kalkbrenner, Herz, Hunten, Döhler, Bertini and co. – must have provided him with the clearest possible sense of what he wished to avoid in his own compositions. So sensitive were Schumann's critical antennae that he was able to distinguish between the potential evident in an apparently conventional display piece like Chopin's op. 2 Variations on 'Là ci darem la mano' and a typically vacuous effusion from a minor figure. He was also able to find virtues in Liszt and Thalberg which raised them above the level of the cliché-ridden productions of the common herd. Nowhere is Schumann's sense of the superiority of German to French or Italian music more evident than in his criticisms of pianistic trash. Yet it is his own mode of piano writing in the 1830s which provides the most telling criticism, for the purely technical challenge is always subordinate to an expressive end, whether delicate or dramatic. There was, in any case, more to his belief in German superiority than this, for dissatisfaction with empty display in the music of other countries was carried over into what he saw as the more serious failure to exploit those larger instrumental forms in which Beethoven and Schubert had been so evidently at home.

Schumann's *annus mirabilis* was 1840, when a lyric muse that had triumphed in the evocations and allusions of the piano works suddenly confronted, and conquered, the lyric texts of Heine, Rückert, Eichendorff and others. With hindsight, that year's achievement seems to embody a productivity born either of sheer desperation or a passionate belief that it was time to move on to the mainstream of symphonic and operatic composition, and that as much small-scale work should therefore be completed while it was still possible. There can be no doubt that the great song-cycles of 1840 – the *Liederkreis* op. 39 and *Dichterliebe* op. 48 in particular – are, to borrow Hugo Wolf's term, the 'swansong' of German Romanticism in its purest early form. Heine's *Dichterliebe* poems stand back from even the degree of skeletal narrative found in *Die schöne Müllerin* and *Die Winterreise*. They deal with feelings in a landscape, in a climate, feelings which swing between tenderness and despair, yet which, despite their intimacy and almost painful reality, do not belong to a character who can be brought to life on a stage. The forms in which these feelings are expressed are small-scale, yet capable of embracing all the necessary variety and intensity. Even so, it is worth noting that at much the same time that Schumann was composing these songs, Wagner was contemplating a work provoked in part by one of Heine's tales. As drama, *Der fliegende Holländer* is all that *Dichterliebe* is not; whereas the song-cycle represents the finest essence of Romanticism, the opera already threatens to break its bonds.

Schumann was not the only master of the early Romantic Lied: the prolific and long-lived Carl Loewe (1796–1869) wrote some of his best pieces between the late 1820s and the early 1840s, including, in his setting of Goethe's *Lynceus, auf Fausts Sternwarte singend* (1833), a song whose superbly shaped and expansive melody makes it one of the greatest songs of all time. But no German composer of the early 1840s was more determined than Schumann to encourage the production of large-scale instrumental compositions in an up-to-date idiom. By that he meant a style that took account of the rhythmic and melodic characteristics of late Beethoven, not just the formal outlines, and by that criterion not even Mendelssohn could be said to have confronted the challenge. The long-established view of Schumann's own music after 1841 is that in general it quite fails to match his earlier achievements, yet one scholar has recently argued persuasively that if we take the Beethoven comparison seriously, putting Schumann's Symphony no. 2 (1845–6) alongside Beethoven's Fifth, we can begin to understand, and even to share, the contemporary enthusiasm for the work (see Newcomb). Nor are the later symphonies negligible: the first movement of the Symphony no. 3 (1850) has an energy, and a relish for purely symphonic argument, which make it Schumann's finest single contribution to the genre in its first post-Beethoven phase; and this is well matched by the poetic yet not merely programmatic slow movement (Feierlich), inspired by a solemn ceremony in Cologne Cathedral. It is also generally accepted that the D minor Symphony – originally no. 2 of 1841, then revised in 1851 as no. 4 – is, overall, as successful a (non-programmatic) symphony as any produced between the death of Beethoven and the completion of Brahms's First. As innumerable analyses have shown, it is the emphasis on thematic cross-reference across all the movements which is new – and which has helped to inspire a frequently misguided belief that such connections can be found in any work worthy of the label 'symphony', if only sufficient analytical ingenuity is exercised. In fact, nineteenth-century music in general – like Schumann's in particular – is rich in contrasts between successful examples of such powerfully forged organicism and those much looser but not less coherent assemblages in which such explicit symphonic unity is of necessity avoided.

Another familiar reason for questioning the quality of Schumann's achievements as a symphonist lies in the nature of his orchestration. Defences of his orchestral textures have been rather less evident than defences of his forms and thematic processes, and his most successful use of the orchestra is probably in the Piano Concerto, where the accompaniment is in general kept so subordinate that the moments of genuine dialogue with the soloist have an attractive air of understatement. In chamber music, the triumph of doubling over dialogue would make the three works for piano and strings completely unacceptable were it not for the freshness of the ideas they contain. And the balance of energy and expressiveness in the best of the string quartets – the A major of 1842 – makes it a satisfying and appealing work, even if the texture is full of pianistic traces. Schumann's best scoring in a chamber work can be found in the Violin Sonata no. 2 (1851), a work whose general success is not weakened by anticipations of Brahms.

There is something heroic in Schumann's persistent tussle with larger forms in his later years, and in his attempt to develop something of Beethoven's uncompromising, even violent spirit in contrast to the 'gracious, well-bred air' of Mendelssohn and others. It was with a single-mindedness perhaps born in part of his own ultimate instability that Schumann strove to further what he judged to be the most vital aspects of the German tradition stemming from Bach and culminating in Beethoven. Maybe he was unwise in failing to recognize that the essence of Beethoven's most radical spirit was still too new to be satisfactorily absorbed, since (in Germany) only with Brahms and Wagner, in their totally different ways, does that spirit begin to act more as a stimulus than an inhibition. But Schumann's own recognition of Brahms, and his touching relationship with that young genius, have all the generosity and excitement of a sense of fulfilment in which there is no bitterness. It is indeed Brahms's work that fulfils Schumann's ideal of a new synthesis in which Classical form and Romantic content challenge and inspire each other. Schumann himself was far less able to understand what Wagner was aiming at – a blind spot all the more comprehensible in view of Schumann's own failings as a dramatic composer.

His large-scale vocal and dramatic works all belong to the period from 1843 to 1853, and have attracted adverse comment more consistently than any other aspect of his output. Today, it is true, such works as *Requiem für Mignon* and *Der Rose Pilgerfahrt* are showing signs of revival: yet Schumann's *Scenes from Goethe's Faust*, despite the fact that it treats its literary source far more respectfully – and sensitively – than Berlioz's *La damnation de Faust*, quite lacks the flair and vitality of the Berlioz. As for Schumann's opera *Genoveva*, the common criticism is not that it is dull through conservatism: it is as throughcomposed as anything of Wagner's of the same period. Its

9 Schumann in October 1853, a few months before the suicide attempt that led to his confinement in an asylum until his death in 1856.

failings are an absence of dramatic conviction, of any real feeling for the theatre. Feeling for the theatre was what Wagner had in abundance. Yet even Wagner could not claim to have invented the genre in which his dramatic works before the *Ring* were cast. Not only, as we have seen, did he acknowledge the genius of Weber; he also, as a young conductor as well as a student of contemporary culture, was familiar with much of the operatic music composed in the years after Weber's death.

The death of Weber in 1826 deprived German Romantic opera of its leading figure, but it also served to bring other composers into greater prominence than they might have achieved had Weber lived on. Weber himself had been well aware of the differences between German opera, as he conceived it, and that of France or Italy, and he was a generous supporter of composers whom he sensed as furthering the national cause. Thus in 1820 he announced 'a genuinely national event' in the appearance of *Heinrich IV und d'Aubigné*, an opera (actually the third), by the young Heinrich Marschner (1795–1861): 'It will be a delight to observe our compatriot's lively and original invention, his fluent melodic gift and rich, studied style. I will even go so far as to prophesy that such a passionate concern with dramatic truth combined with such a profoundly emotional nature will produce a dramatic composer worthy of our highest respect'. A 'rich,

43

studied style' and a 'concern with dramatic truth' were, in Weber's view, the principal differences between German opera (and those works of French *opéra comique* which, as already indicated, strongly influenced developments in Germany) and inferior, essentially Italian works. German Romantic opera also showed a preference for certain types of subject: political themes, as explored in various 'rescue operas', were the most 'realistic'; otherwise, there was an emphasis on the legendary, the exotic, the supernatural – not least the impact of the supernatural on an ordinary human situation. Such subjects were explored before Wagner by, among others, E. T. A. Hoffmann, Spohr, Marschner and Lortzing. Indeed, pre-Wagnerian Romantic opera is conveniently framed by two treatments of the Undine legend, by Hoffmann (1816) and Lortzing (1845); the latter work is a particularly attractive example of how an essentially lyrical language, while far less forceful or forward-looking than that Wagner himself was employing in the 1840s, can still create a strong and effective dramatic atmosphere.

Interesting though it is to observe the extent to which composers after Weber continued to explore those features of his work which now seem most significant as anticipations of Wagner's techniques – of leitmotif, form and orchestration – it is idle to pretend that any of them consistently matched Weber's powers of invention or degree of dramatic conviction. German composers were most successful in lighter, lyrical, more comic vein: Lortzing's *Zar und Zimmermann* (1837) and Nicolai's *Die lustigen Weiber von Windsor* (1849) are two relatively familiar examples. Of the many attempts at more weighty, or simply more sinister, works, none between *Euryanthe* and *Der fliegende Holländer* is more impressive than Marschner's *Hans Heiling* (1833). Taken all in all, however, there was not enough in German Romantic opera after Weber to give Wagner the basic materials for his own dramas. And Wagner had the honesty to acknowledge the importance of quite different composers – even Auber – when reviewing the origins of his own mature style. As a consequence of the great leap forward made by Wagner between *Rienzi* and *Der fliegende Holländer*, German symphonic music of the 1840s was to look even more inept and second rate. Until well after 1850, the problem of the Beethoven legacy was to remain unsolved, and in the process of solving it Romanticism itself would be transformed.

CHAPTER FOUR

'True passion and emotion':
the Italian alternative, from Paganini to Donizetti

'In his compositions and performance there is a strange mixture of the highest genius, childishness and tastelessness, so that one feels alternately attracted and repelled'. This was Spohr's reaction to hearing Paganini play in Kassel in 1830, and it vividly suggests the German musician's mixture of admiration and dislike in the face of such a phenomenon. Niccolò Paganini (1782–1840) was not heard outside Italy until 1828, and his international career was finished six years later. Yet despite the relative brevity of that career, and despite the fact that his compositions are far from initiating a radical break with Classical forms, it is he of all musicians who personifies the most lurid notions of Romanticism. No other string player was able to challenge his supremacy, and it took a supreme artist in another medium, Heinrich Heine, to paint, in one of his essays, an appropriately arresting verbal portrait. 'He dressed from head to foot in black. His body, racked with pain, was slowly wasting away from syphilis. He glided rather than walked across the stage – like a menacing vulture gently floating into position to consume its prey. His eyes had receded deep into their sockets, and this, together with his waxen complexion, gave him a spectral appearance which was enhanced by the dark-blue glasses he sometimes wore. The mercury prescribed for his *morbo gallico* had attacked his stomach and rotted his jawbone, causing his teeth to decay and fall out and his mouth to disappear into his chin. When Paganini played, the macabre impression was that of a bleached skull with a violin tucked under its chin. His very name ("little pagan") symbolized the satanic aura which surrounded his personality' (*Florentine Nights*).

However meretricious Paganini's methods, and music, may seem to a later age, he was able to impress the greater talents of his time by his personal qualities as well as by his musicianship. Berlioz, although he never heard him play, declared that 'his melody is in the great Italian tradition, but it generally moves with a more passionate life than the melody met with even in the finest pages of the dramatic composers among his compatriots. His harmony is always clear, simple, and of extraordinary sonority'. Of course, Berlioz benefited not just from Paganini's commissioning of *Harold en Italie* in 1833 but also from a gift of 20,000 francs in 1838, accompanied by a fulsome eulogy: 'Beethoven being dead, only Berlioz can make him live again.' Already, in 1832, Paganini's example had inspired Liszt to begin the task of composing really challenging virtuoso music for the piano. Yet in later years Liszt was to comment sententiously on Paganini's 'egotism' and 'self-serving virtuosity', and express the hope that 'the artist of the future' would be 'the means of virtuosity, and not its end'. Spohr would doubtless have agreed.

Paganini was not a typical Italian composer for the simple reason that he did not write operas. He was therefore a less significant influence on the emergence of Romanticism out of Classicism than Rossini, whose style dominated operatic music until the early 1850s. Yet Rossini (1792–1868) was never more than a partial, even reluctant Romantic, and Italian opera in the late 1820s and early 1830s reflected that reluctance, making it, on the whole, less forwardlooking than its German counterpart. And despite the appearance of new talent – Bellini with *Il pirata* (1827), Donizetti with *Anna Bolena* (1830) and Verdi with *Oberto* (1839) – Rossinian formal precedents remained in large part unchallenged until after 1850, not least, no doubt, because they showed themselves well able to take on Romantic colouring.

The challenge posed, and the example set, by Rossini were all the more tantalizing in view of the fact that his last – grand – opera, written for Paris (*Guillaume Tell*, 1829), was so successful an advance into a new theatrical world, whose lessons were still being learned as late as 1867, in Verdi's last great offering to the French capital, *Don Carlos*. Several historians have suggested that the composer most strongly influenced by Rossini's later works was a relatively minor one, Saverio Mercadante (1795–1870), whose 'reformist' aim, evident in *Il giuramento* (1837) and several subsequent operas, was the honourable, progressive one of not allowing musical conventions to dictate the form and progress of the drama. Regrettably, Mercadante did not keep up the good work, and it was Donizetti whose operas proved to have the vitality and adaptability to withstand Verdi's assault in the century's third quarter. To argue that only in the later Donizetti, and in Verdi, were the lessons of Rossini's late work fully learned is to recognize that Meyerbeer, the most successful of all

10 Paganini in action. Sketch by Landseer (*c.* 1831) of the archetypal Romantic virtuoso.

grand opera composers in Paris after 1830, failed to profit from the Rossinian example in *Guillaume Tell*. Meyerbeer (to be discussed in Chapter Five) was an important figure in the development of Romanticism in opera, as his earlier, by no means un-Rossinian, Italian works show – especially the last, *Il crociato in Egitto* (1824). In Italy itself, however, it was first Bellini and then Donizetti who did most to transform the 'Rossini Era' into the 'Romantic Era'.

Of course, to the likes of Berlioz and Wagner, Rossini was – comic opera aside – deserving of utter contempt. Raging against the Rossini 'cult', Berlioz argued that 'my wrath was all the greater because the whole style of the new school was diametrically opposed to that of Gluck and Spontini. I could imagine nothing more sublimely beautiful and true than the works of those great masters. By contrast, Rossini's melodic cynicism, his contempt for dramatic expression and good sense, his endless repetition of a single form of cadence, his eternal puerile crescendo and brutal bass drum, exasperated me to

47

such a point that I was blind to the brilliant qualities of his genius even in his masterpiece, the *Barber*, exquisitely scored though it is.' For Wagner, 'with Rossini the real life of opera comes to an end . . . All pretence of drama had been scrupulously swept away . . . the history of opera, since Rossini, is at bottom nothing else but the history of operatic melody.' Even those critics who most fiercely defend Bellini's claim to be taken seriously as an opera composer, and as a Romantic, are likely to concede that it is as a melodist that he is supreme: Wagner himself testified to the 'true passion and emotion' of Bellini's melodies, and Berlioz pointed to deeper virtues as a composer in his generally hostile account of *I Capuleti e i Montecchi*, commenting that Bellini was at least able 'to extract something memorable' from the most unpromising material.

Vincenzo Bellini's life – 1801–35 – was of course too brief for him to make as powerful an impact on the development of Italian opera as Rossini. Yet he was able to create a decisive change of emphasis. Already in *Il pirata* (1827) he was moving towards a style that depended less than Rossini's on the grand gesture and flamboyant

11 The vulnerable Romantic heroine. A scene from a 19th-century production of Bellini's *La sonnambula*.

vocal virtuosity, and while neither *La sonnambula* nor *Norma* (both 1831) abandoned all Rossinian, or Classical, qualities, they helped to consolidate his reputation and prepare for the more adventurous orchestration and harmony, as well as the freer forms, found in his last two operas, *Beatrice di Tenda* (1833) and *I puritani* (1835). Perhaps the most forward-looking and influential feature of *Norma* is its ending with the death of the heroine. With Bellini, happy endings become the exception, and had he lived longer his success – he was able to make his living entirely from opera commissions after 1827, and was able to insist on a longer period for the composition of his operas than was normal in those harshly commercial times – and his feeling for innovation, fuelled by his awareness of developments in France, might well have led to much greater things. As it was, Bellini was able to provide only the Prelude to Italian Romantic opera. In an interesting assessment written in 1885, Eduard Hanslick – for whom Bellini was the Italian Spohr – summed up his career as follows: 'Bellini was naive even in his trivialities. He was one of the last of the naive masters. His limited vocabulary was often inadequate for the scope of his emotions, but the emotions were genuine and flowed straight from the heart. With a God-given, if severely restricted talent, he gave to *Norma* and the somewhat weaker *La sonnambula* the best that was in him. There are excellent things side by side with poor and outmoded stuff. But who since Bellini has written a melody with the sweet, long breath of "Casta diva", or a song more expressive in its ultimate simplicity than that of the final duet "Qual cor tradisti", or a soulful melody so plastically effective as the "Padre, tu piangi" in the last finale? One of the best pieces of music Wagner ever wrote, the second finale of *Tannhäuser*, points unmistakably to the final scene of *Norma* as its model in the effective climax, "Ich fleh' für ihn".'

Hanslick is right to point to an instance of Bellini's wider influence. Locally, that influence was a good deal more crucial, for a combination of the example of *Il pirata* and of Rossini's later French operas did much to stimulate the development of Donizetti's style. Gaetano Donizetti (1797–1848) has been most widely praised for his comedies, *L'elisir d'amore* (1832) and *Don Pasquale* (1842). But it was in his serious operas that he made his most sustained and influential contribution to Romantic music, extending from the 'semiseria' *Emilia di Liverpool* (1824) to *Dom Sébastien* (1843), nineteen years and fifty-three operas later.

Donizetti's leading twentieth-century apologist, William Ashbrook, has claimed that he 'was a composer of the theatre in a sense that neither Rossini nor Bellini was; that is, he tried always to bring music and drama into a closer, more direct conjunction than his great contemporaries'. For those who see early Romantic excellence primarily in terms of poetic refinement (Chopin, Schumann) on the one hand, and preparation for Wagner's 'symphonic' music drama on the other, such a claim is likely to be dismissed as arrant special pleading: indeed, the only comment in Ashbrook's long study of which they are likely to approve are the quoted words of Théophile Gautier (whose poems were so superbly set by Berlioz in *Les nuits d'été*, 1840–41), in his review of *La favorite* (December 1840): 'It contains facility, happily conceived melodies, passages well written for the voice, a certain éclat, but one also finds in it at each step shopworn melodies and threadbare, trivial phrases; a hasty negligence which one forgives in Italy, but which is inappropriate to the more serious habits of our [Parisian] lyric theatres.'

Judged by the purely musical standards of Berlioz, Chopin, Schumann – and even the earlier Liszt – at their best, Donizetti's music may well seem thin and limited. Nevertheless, the attempt to 'bring music and drama into a closer, more direct conjunction' is undeniable: it involves a more progressive attitude to form than is found in Rossini and Bellini, as well as a willingness to tackle subjects which, by the standards of the time, were controversial. Donizetti was by no means content to accept the operatic status quo uncritically; operas like *Lucrezia Borgia* (1833) and *Maria Stuarda* (1834) may seem mild enough today, but in the 1830s they were certain to provoke the censors, and only a composer with strong beliefs in their dramatic validity would have attempted them. It was the desire to escape the worst restrictions of Italian censorship that encouraged Donizetti to move to Paris in the mid-1830s: there, composers, like other artists, were in general more highly regarded than elsewhere, and although, as Chapter Five will show, Paris was not particularly kind to its greatest 'native' Romantic, Berlioz, it offered unrivalled opportunities to a composer whose works were more in tune with commercial and social realities. Nevertheless, it would be wrong to assume that Donizetti only became interested in formal innovation and more challenging dramatic themes after his arrival in Paris. *Anna Bolena* (1830, first performed in Milan) is usually

12 Giuditta Pasta (1797–1865) in the title role of Donizetti's *Anna Bolena* (1830). At the time she was Europe's leading coloratura soprano, specializing in operas by Rossini, Bellini and Donizetti.

regarded as the crucial turning point in a career that had begun twenty-eight operas earlier, in 1816, with the one-act 'scena lyrica' *Il Pigmalione*. *Anna Bolena* is notable for its eager grasp of every opportunity for what now seem the essentials of Italian Romantic melodrama, and commentators have emphasized a shift of dramatic focus from the more reflective, lyrical type of aria to the duet, in which an element of action, of conflict between the participants, may be represented. The duet for Anna and Seymour near the beginning of Act II is a good example of this new formal scope and freedom, and while the musical emphasis may still be on vocal melody, the accompanying harmony promotes expressive intensity by exploring a relatively wide range of regions within the basic tonality. Balancing the moments of confrontation and conflict, there are equally vivid representations of pathos, as in the final scene, where once again the form is flexible and continuous, and relatively short, lyrical arioso carries the essence of the musical expression.

The importance of these aspects of *Anna Bolena* is in no way reduced by awareness of the opera's debts to Bellini's *Il pirata* or by the realization that its Romantic qualities had been foreshadowed in earlier works of Donizetti's own – *Emilia di Liverpool* (1824), *Gabriella di Vergy* (1826) – or indeed, that *Anna* itself actually contains music adapted from earlier operas. As, relatively speaking, a great leap forwards, *Anna Bolena* also owes much to the unusual quality of Romani's libretto, in the setting of which Donizetti responded with particular force to the opportunities for pathos in the tragic dénouement. More important still is the fact that, after the success of *Anna Bolena*, Donizetti continued his search for new ways of exploiting and modifying the conventions of the genre within which he worked. The notion of extended scenes built from distinct but connected elements, as opposed to strictly separate 'numbers', was of course central to all Romantic opera, and in Donizetti's case it seems clear that he learned to appreciate its value most directly from the work of his teacher J. S. Mayr. (The importance of such a formal concept to grand opera, and the work of Meyerbeer in particular, after 1830, will be discussed in Chapter Five.) But there were other avenues to be explored as well. For example, in *Torquato Tasso* (1833) Donizetti sought to go beyond the combination of tragic and *buffo* elements found in the *opera semiseria* to explore the conjunction of more extreme contrasts – a more heroic tragedy and a broader comedy – than was normal for the time. The result may not be completely successful, but it does anticipate an approach Verdi was to tackle in *La forza del destino* nearly thirty years later.

To criticize Donizetti for not advancing more radically still into the world of truly throughcomposed music drama is to condemn him for not taking an even more lofty attitude (or for affecting total indifference) to contemporary commercial and artistic realities than he actually did. Even when opera was moving away from completely separate numbers to compound scenes music publishers still wished to satisfy the strong public demand for separate excerpts – one reason why we find Wagner (in Paris in 1840) arranging items from operas by Donizetti and Halévy for piano and cornet. In the world of Italian opera only Verdi, after his early successes, would be able to challenge such commercial considerations, and none of his operas, even the late masterpieces, can be said wholly to dispense with the traditional distinctions between such basic formal elements as aria and ensemble.

Where Donizetti achieved considerable success was in the range of possibilities he was able to exploit within the existing conventions. He introduced an aria form in which the normal slow cantabile/fast cabaletta scheme is replaced by a form in which the 'cabaletta' is actually slower than the cantabile which precedes it – for example, Chevreuse's aria from Act I of *Maria di Rohan* (1843). Such examples are of course exceptional, and *Maria di Rohan* is Donizetti's last opera but one: but they do give priority to the drama rather than to possibilities for vocal display. In fact it is Act III of *Maria di Rohan* which William Ashbrook regards as probably the composer's finest single achievement. The work was written for Vienna, and its subject, a Romantic melodrama of guilty passions, duels, jealousy and retribution is of the type – remote alike from magical and political subjects – which Donizetti generally preferred. Maria is the last of his long line of tragic heroines, and the opera represents the culmination of the composer's search for ways of ensuring deeper and more vivid characterization.

Vocal display is certainly not excluded from Act III of this work: nor are those sectional divisions and clear cadences at the end of episodes to allow for applause (or catcalls). But – provided we set aside unrealistic expectations about the total transformation of convention – there is an economy and an intensity in the musical fabric which bring an undeniable conviction to the drama. And it is certainly not farfetched to see in Donizetti's constant search for

13 Donizetti at work, 1840: the year in which *La fille du régiment* was first performed, and *La favorite* composed. He is portrayed writing two operas simultaneously: comic with his right hand, serious with his left.

practicable innovation, and his growing preoccupation in his later years with the darker emotions of guilt, jealousy and remorse, as well as in the richer harmony and orchestration of his later works for Paris and Vienna, a manner closer to middle-period Verdi than to Bellini, or even to Donizetti's own earlier work. From atmospheric orchestral introductions which suggest Schumann or even early Wagner to cumulative ensembles which might end acts without the conventional *stretta*, Donizetti consistently sought for greater flexibility and expressiveness. It is even possible to argue, as Winton Dean has convincingly done, that the relative absence of Donizettian influence on the early Verdi is a measure of the older composer's greater experience and subtlety. The most interesting resemblances occur later, and although from *Rigoletto* (1851) onwards Verdi forged powerfully ahead, the links can (as already suggested) be traced at least as far as *La forza del destino* (1862).

Italian Romantic opera before the mature Verdi was written under essentially eighteenth-century conditions. Factors like the availability of singers, not to mention the (conservative) tastes of the public, meant that the possibility of changing an aria at the last minute mattered more than the preservation of a forward-looking formal scheme of compound scenes with emphasis on atmospheric orchestral episodes and duets in which characters boldly confronted each other rather than indulged in contests of vocal virtuosity. Recent research – Budden, Rosselli – has emphasized the realities of a world in which composers had to compete for contracts in an utterly commercial market: a world in which the composer who finished an opera most speedily stood the best chance of winning further commissions. Such a situation is hardly conducive to the creation of profound or sophisticated art, or to the contemplation of those qualities of structure and expression likely to lead to great Romantic art. And so admiration of Donizetti for the degree to which he was able to surmount such circumstances must be coupled with relief that, during the 1840s, Verdi began to develop the skills, and to acquire the means – and the will – to change them.

CHAPTER FIVE

'Beethoven being dead ...':
Berlioz and Romanticism in France

In February 1840 Hector Berlioz (1803–69) wrote bitterly that 'M. Donizetti seems to treat us like a conquered country; it is a veritable invasion. One can no longer speak of the opera houses of Paris, but only of the opera houses of M. Donizetti.' Donizetti himself responded with sympathy in a letter to a friend: 'Berlioz? Poor man . . . he wrote an opera, it was whistled at, he is writing symphonies and they are whistled at, he writes articles . . . they are laughed at . . . and everyone is laughing and everyone is whistling. I alone feel compassion for him . . . he is right . . . he has to avenge himself.' Critical appreciation of Berlioz in the twentieth century has been accompanied by a good deal of discussion of the 'Classical' aspects of his style. Yet in his own time the emphasis seems to have been almost wholly on the radical and disturbing: for Schumann 'his melodies are characterized by such an intensity, almost to the individual note, that they, like many old folk songs, can hardly bear a harmonic accompaniment'. Much later, in 1879, Verdi commented: 'There are certainly marvellous things in his work. Lofty inspiration, but his compositions are contorted, confused and stilted.' And three years earlier Verdi had described Berlioz as 'a poor sick man, furious with everybody, acrimonious and malicious. He had a great talent, and a feeling for instrumentation . . . He lacked moderation. And he lacked the calm and, I would say, the equilibrium that produces complete works of art. He always went to extremes, even when creating something praiseworthy.'

Berlioz's importance as an orchestral innovator, and as the author of a famous study of instrumentation (1843) has never been doubted. The development of the art of orchestration during the Romantic period involved technical changes in the instruments themselves, bringing greater strength and brilliance to string tone and greater flexibility and variety to the wind. There were new, often exotic instruments: E flat clarinet, bass clarinet, bass (and Wagner) tuba, celesta, saxophone. But, the Romantic composer, as distinct from his

14 A drawing of Antoine (Adolph) Sax, the celebrated instrument maker and inventor.

Classical predecessor, was unlikely to have an orchestra under his direct control for long periods, and when he did, as with Liszt at Weimar, he might well find the situation less than ideal: the première of *Lohengrin* in 1850 was given with an orchestra of fewer than forty players. Even so, the orchestra was a powerful means of promoting the poetic essence of Romantic musical communication, and the increasing importance of public concerts, and the emergence of the conductor as the focus of an interpretation rather than simply a mechanism for its efficient presentation, both contributed greatly to this end.

Nevertheless, it was primarily as a composer that Berlioz himself wished to function, and it was his misfortune to develop such a challenging, apparently immoderate idiom at a time when opera, the pre-eminent musical medium in Paris, was dominated by foreigners very different from those earlier immigrants – Gluck, Spontini – whom Berlioz himself so admired. Berlioz's opinion of Rossini has already been quoted (pp. 47–8). As for Meyerbeer, his view was that 'the pressure he exerts on managers, artists and critics and consequently on the Paris public, at least as much by his immense wealth as by his genuine eclectic talent, makes all serious success at the

56

Opéra virtually impossible.' Elsewhere, Berlioz wrote bitterly that 'the author of *Le prophète* not only has the good luck to have talent, he also has the talent to have good luck.' Yet he also accused the Opéra of being 'madly in love with mediocrity' and declared despairingly that 'in my country there are circumstances which even the most unusual musical genius, the most undisputed, the most astounding, cannot overcome'. The reference is to Paganini, but the relevance extends to Berlioz himself. From 1831, with the first performance of *Robert le diable*, grand opera in general, and Meyerbeer in particular, stood for everything that Berlioz most despised, and historians have sometimes found it difficult to balance the understandable Berliozian bias against a more objective appraisal of the grand opera phenomenon itself.

Soon after his arrival in Paris, in December 1831, Chopin wrote to a friend: 'If ever magnificence was seen in a theatre I doubt whether it reached the level of splendour shown in *Robert le Diable*, the very latest five-act opera of Meyerbeer . . . It is a masterpiece of the modern school . . . On the stage there's a diorama in which, towards the end, you see the inside of a church and the whole church itself at Christmas or Easter all lit up, with monks and congregation seated, with censers, and what is more, with a grand organ, whose sound . . . enchants and amazes one and practically drowns the whole orchestra. No one will ever stage anything like it. Meyerbeer has made himself immortal.' The easy, and not uncommon, twentieth-century response to this is that it was precisely the concern with spectacle (at the expense of substance) that has made Meyerbeer (1791–1864) one of the most mortal of all the prominent Romantics. After all, there may be sardonic undertones to Chopin's words, and there were other sceptics: Mendelssohn, also writing about *Robert le diable*, commented that 'there is an expenditure of all possible means of producing stage effects that I never saw equalled. All who can sing, dance, or act in Paris, sing, dance, and act on this occasion. The subject is romantic, that is, the devil appears in the piece (that is quite sufficient romance and imagination for the Parisians). It is very bad, however; and were it not for two brilliant scenes of seduction it would produce no effect whatever.'

Even before Wagner, evidently, it was possible to see Meyerbeer as essentially meretricious, and there is clearly little point in approaching the collaboration between Meyerbeer, the librettist Scribe, and the impresario who masterminded the emergence of grand opera, Louis

Véron, with the lofty aims of the *Gesamtkunstwerk* in mind. Yet the two are by no means polar opposites, not least because both are manifestations of the Romantic spirit in the theatre. Victor Hugo, in the preface to his play *Cromwell* (1827), had called for an 'illusion of reality' in drama, and the change of emphasis in opera, away from unhistorical characters and unrealistic settings, as well as unspectacular productions, had begun with Auber's *La muette de Portici* (1828) and Rossini's *Guillaume Tell* (1829).

Meyerbeer, whose *Robert le diable* was originally conceived with spoken dialogue in 1827, was able to capitalize on Rossini's indolence, and Auber's evident preference for *opéra comique* (he produced no fewer than thirty-four such works between 1813 and 1869, mostly in association with Scribe). The immediate appeal of *Robert* was doubtless due in large part to its evident debts (Spontini, Weber), and the hostility to Meyerbeer, of Berlioz and Wagner in particular, centred on what was seen as his unrivalled, even enviable, ability to exploit current fads and fashions. As Wagner put it: 'Meyerbeer in Italy composed operas *à la* Rossini, just till the larger wind of Paris commenced to chop, and Auber and Rossini with their *Muette* and their *Tell* blew the new gale into a storm. With one bound was Meyerbeer in Paris! There he found, however, in the Frenchified Weber (need I recall *Robin des Bois?*) and the be-Berliozed Beethoven, certain elements to which neither Auber nor Rossini had paid attention, as lying too far out of their way, but which Meyerbeer in virtue of his cosmopolitan capacity knew very well to valuate. He summed up all his overhearings in one monstrous hybrid phrase, whose strident outcry rendered Rossini and Auber suddenly inaudible: "Robert", the grim "Devil", set his clutches on them all!' And Wagner's honestly partial conclusion was that 'he became the weathercock of European music, the vane that always veers at first uncertain with the shift of wind, and comes to a standstill only when the wind itself has settled on its quarter.'

Supreme opportunist Meyerbeer may have been, but he did not follow up *Robert le diable* with a long string of similar works: *Les Huguenots* (1836), *Le prophète* (1849) and *L'africaine* (1865) were his only other grand operas, and it was a setting of a Scribe libretto by another composer, *La juive* by Jacques Halévy (1835), which apparently provided not only the ultimate demonstration of the scenic skills of the Paris Opéra but also led to widespread fears that

15 Grand opera at its most spectacular. A crowded stage in the Coronation scene of Meyerbeer's *Le prophète* (1849), shown in a contemporary engraving.

musical substance was being sacrificed to mere spectacle. Whatever its musical failings, *La juive* is a good demonstration of Scribe's contribution to Romantic drama as something more than lurid tales of the designs of the devil on humanity. Like *La muette de Portici*, *Guillaume Tell* and *Les Huguenots*, its essential theme is persecution, and heroic resistance against tyranny. It was through such subjects that Scribe reflected those more liberal ideals and attitudes evident in French Romanticism after 1830, and played an important part in helping French opera to contribute to the Romantic activity of criticizing current social evils and proposing improvements. It is not difficult to see connections between such developments and the later work of both Verdi and Wagner.

Nevertheless, even Scribe's most devoted admirers would not claim that his texts were much more than efficient vessels into which music was to be poured: the drama would become convincing, if at all, through musical means. What was needed, to match the powerful subject-matter and the spectacular staging, was the big effect and the large span, and Meyerbeer's outstanding achievement was, as William L. Crosten has noted, 'the organization of music into large units of sound corresponding to the dramatic scheme of presenting an action through a series of great tableaux'. As a result the focus shifts from the single aria, from lyrical reflection, and from the alternation of song and speech found in *opéra comique*, to large throughcomposed and cumulative schemes such as the rondo-type form that ends Act I of *Robert le diable*.

Meyerbeer's skills as a musical architect were undeniable, but architecture is not the whole story in opera; one serious consequence of the new emphasis on action and incident was a narrowing of emotional range, and the appearance of what Verdi identified in *Le prophète* as 'a wearisome heaviness'. Another defect was seized on by Schumann, writing of *Les Huguenots*: 'That famous, deadly, bleating, unbecoming rhythm, that runs through practically all the themes of the opera'. Crosten underlines this weakness: 'In place of real psychological penetration we are too often given only the external clatter of a scene.' No wonder Berlioz, with his vision of a sublime music drama derived from Virgil and Gluck, was bitter about the kind of public that admired such relative vapidity, and the kind of composer capable of providing it. Even Berlioz admitted to finding 'grandeur and truth' in *Les Huguenots*, however, and in providing such a clear indication to both Wagner and Verdi of the need to fill the new, large forms with more powerful, compelling music, the Meyerbeerian grand opera made a particularly vital contribution to the nineteenth-century evolution of the form.

In an impassioned statement of belief which also reads like an attack on current standards and conventions in the opera house, Berlioz declared that 'we must show the warmest regard for theatrical compositions in which music is respected and passion nobly expressed, and in which are displayed common sense, naturalness, plain truth, grandeur without bombast and strength without brutality ... A work in good taste, truly musical and coming from the heart ... why, in our times of exaggeration, vociferation, dislocation, mechanism, and manikinism, we must adore it, throw a veil over its defects, and put it on so high a pedestal that the mud splashing around it cannot reach it . . . The cause of great art, of pure and true art, is compromised by the theatre; but it will triumph in the theatre itself if we artists defend it and fight for it with unremitting strength and constancy.' There was of course more to the musical situation in Paris after 1830 than the apparent ascendancy of Meyerbeer; indeed, as recent research has shown, Meyerbeer was by no means the central figure of the French musical scene, and even he was not always able to do exactly as he liked (see Roberts). In any case, Berlioz was not just at odds with the Opéra, but his idols – Virgil, Shakespeare, Gluck, Beethoven, Goethe – also enshrine the kind of fundamental contrasts that can place Classical constraints on Romantic extravagance, and offer the lesson that passionate emotion may be the more powerful when expressed through controlled though never merely 'simple' forms.

So even if the discovery of Berlioz-like qualities in earlier French music, like that of his teacher Lesueur, reinforces his 'legitimacy' at the expense of his originality, this cannot be considered as rendering redundant all reference to those essential links with the Classic and early Romantic 'mainstream', including Schubert. Yet the link with Beethoven has always seemed the most significant. Wagner may have been fantasizing when, in 1841, he exclaimed that 'from our Germany the spirit of Beethoven has wafted over to him, and there must have been times when Berlioz wished he were German'; after all, in the same essay Wagner also suggested that 'Berlioz seems to enjoy his isolation and stubbornly tries to maintain it'. Yet, as we have already seen (p. 46), for that archetypal Romantic, Paganini, Berlioz was not simply a modern master but the heir of Beethoven – and from such a view there has stemmed as much misconception as insight.

If it is difficult to evaluate exactly how important Beethoven's residence, and acceptance, in Vienna was to the nature and extent of his achievement, it is even harder to determine how different Berlioz's life and work might have been had he found a large and enthusiastic audience for his music in Paris – or, for that matter, a small but dedicated and generous circle of admirers and patrons. His life-story reads like that of a prototypical Romantic Wanderer, although the honour he lacked in his own country was not lacking elsewhere, and the loneliness his travels forced on him was compensated for, at least in part, by strong professional friendships and family ties. While the most spectacular episodes of his earlier life might suggest an exaggerated nonconformity, a flamboyant eccentricity, the depth of his attachments and the sheer persistence with which he pursued his musical vocation bring more than a touch of genuine heroism to the story of his life and work. He was much more than a musical corsair, and there was much more to his music than visions of witches' sabbaths and rides to the abyss. As a conductor he was one of the very first to regard the composer's text as something not to be decorated, or truncated, at will: 'To modify the music one sings, or the book one is translating, without saying a word about it to the man who wrote it only after much thought, is to commit a shocking breach of trust – unfaithful interpreters are libellers and assassins'.

Born into a professional family – his father was a doctor in the Isère region, not far from Grenoble – Berlioz's early musical explorations were certainly not stifled, and although life in the provinces deprived him of the kind of musical experiences only the capital could offer, the Alpine vistas of the local landscape provided a stimulating backdrop to his development. The family was not a musical one, and it was literature which provided the first, formative experience: 'It was Virgil who first found the way to my heart and opened my budding imagination, by speaking to me of epic passions for which instinct had prepared me.' As Berlioz states in his *Memoirs*, his father would not allow him to learn the piano (flute, flageolet and guitar were permitted), and paternal hostility would erupt with a vengeance when Berlioz decided to abandon his own medical studies in Paris for music. According to the *Memoirs*, a prime cause of this fateful choice was a performance of Gluck's *Iphigénie en Tauride* at the Opéra. Berlioz already knew Gluck's music from the scores in the library of the Conservatoire: 'I copied them and learned them by heart, I went without sleep because of them and forgot to eat and drink.' It was another 'epic passion', and from that point on, no discouragement would prevent the young Berlioz from pursuing his obsession: 'As useless and dangerous for another will to oppose mine when it is thoroughly roused as it is to try to prevent gunpowder from exploding by compression.'

With such determination it is perhaps surprising that Berlioz should have been willing to submit to academic instruction. He certainly did not suppress his own already considerable desire to compose in the early 1820s, but he also took lessons at the Conservatoire, entering that institution officially as late as 1826, when he was already twenty-two, and was completing his first opera, *Les francs-juges*. In 1830, after much conflict and crisis, Berlioz won the Prix de Rome, but that academic accolade was more than usually ironic in view of the way in which his life and work had developed since 1826. It can also be argued that had Berlioz stayed in Paris at that time he might quite rapidly have achieved the success and stability which, on his return from Italy in 1832, eluded him.

It may reduce biography from concision to caricature to say that the three most crucial influences on Berlioz after Virgil and Gluck all entered his experience in the late 1820s: Shakespeare (especially Harriet Smithson in *Othello*), Beethoven (especially the symphonies) and Goethe (especially *Faust*). But little of real importance is omitted if the consequences of these various passions are traced through the remaining forty years of his life. The Shakespearean passion was particularly profound, of course, and the extraordinary story of Berlioz's relationship with Harriet Smithson cannot be outdone in a century of many harrowing and turbulent liaisons. The bald facts are that the couple did not marry until 1833, after a six-year 'on–off' courtship during which Berlioz was diverted into an even more tempestuous affair with the young pianist Camille Moke. After marriage, there were approximately six years of relative content, but then came disillusion, separation, Harriet's long final illness and her death in 1854. Ultimately, it is the sheer length of Berlioz's involvement with Harriet that seems so remarkable (although the length may simply have been due to the amount of time they spent apart – Berlioz had a close relationship with the singer Marie Recio for many years before Harriet's death); and his involvement with Shakespeare was even longer, accounting for two major and very different works, the dramatic symphony *Roméo et Juliette* (1839) and the opera *Béatrice et Bénédict* (1860–62), as well as such smaller pieces as the overture *Le roi Lear* (1841), *La morte d'Ophélie* (1842) and the *Marche funèbre pour la dernière scène d'Hamlet* (1844).

Berlioz did not hesitate to link Shakespeare and Beethoven in his personal pantheon: 'Beethoven opened before me a new world of music, as Shakespeare had revealed a new universe of poetry.' Exactly what that new world contained, and what use Berlioz himself made of it, is not so easily determined, however, for that willingness to submit to academic instruction, noted above, does not alter the fact that it makes most sense to see him as his own most important teacher, using the scores of Gluck, Spontini, Beethoven and others as his primers. Musical analysis is never more tentative than when attempting to provide conclusive proof of the analyst's intuitions about the influence of a great master on a young master's development. For example, whatever the documentary evidence of Berlioz's avowed intention of using a Beethovenian framework for his *Symphonie fantastique*, the establishment of direct links between the two composers is as difficult as it is – or may seem – irrelevant. Yet recent research tends to confirm that Beethoven's demonstrable influence on Berlioz is relatively slight, even in the piece which establishes Beethovenian associations most clearly, the *Lear* overture. And that is hardly surprising, if we accept that for Berlioz melody was a more fundamental expressive and structural tool than harmony, or form in any broader sense. That in itself scarcely marks out Berlioz as a special case in the world of early Romanticism, but allied with other factors it does help to account for his remarkable originality, and the widespread disagreement – which still persists – about the quality and content of his achievement.

Berlioz's writings are full of the bitterness of a creator who knows his worth and feels himself out of both time and place: 'With our culture as it is, and under our form of government, the more of an artist a man is the more he will have to endure; the grander and more original his work, the harsher the penalty he must pay; the loftier his inspiration soars, the harder the blear-eyed multitude to discern it.' On his return to France from Italy in 1832 he soon encountered that incomprehension that would determine and dominate the rest of his life. One of the earlier chapters of the *Memoirs* is entitled 'Calamity! – I become a critic', and that calamity was such that, during the 1830s, at least, he was regarded by Parisians more as critic than as composer. Abroad, his distinction as both composer and conductor was increasingly acknowledged, but the long saga of his attempts to promote and perform his own works in Paris itself led to the kind of bitter denunciations quoted above. After all, his compositions of the period 1834–46, including the opera *Benvenuto Cellini*, the *Grande messe des morts*, *Roméo et Juliette* and *La damnation de Faust* (deriving from the early *8 Scènes de Faust*, 1828–9), were his most radical – if also his most Romantic – and while the enthusiasm of Liszt and Wagner, among others, was some compensation, it was still a bitter blow that the successes of Meyerbeer and Halévy should make it impossible for Berlioz himself to succeed where it mattered most, at the Opéra: as another chapter title in the *Memoirs* has it: 'Varieties of spleen – isolation!'

1848, when Berlioz wrote the preface to his *Memoirs*, was a year of revolution in Europe, after which the social and cultural atmosphere changed in France. Even so, little happened to change Berlioz's belief that 'I belong to a nation which has ceased to be interested in the higher manifestations of the mind: whose only god is the golden calf.' And he went on to assert that 'we are witnessing the triumph of industrialism in Art, raised to power by the crude popular instincts to which it panders'. Berlioz's bitterness was perhaps the greater in view of the fact that he did actually attempt a collaboration with Scribe during the 1840s. He worked on an opera called *La nonne sanglante* (based on M. G. Lewis's notorious Gothick novel *The Monk*), and some of the music survives. But the similarity to *Robert le diable*, as well as the poor quality of Scribe's verse, combined to deter Berlioz from completion, although around the time when the opera was abandoned, in 1847, he actually discussed with Scribe a possible staging of *La damnation de Faust*, to be called *Méphistophélès*.

Berlioz's outburst about 'crude popular instincts' may seem surprising; he was no more anti-elitist than the other great Romantics, but nor was he in sympathy with the kind of music which, after 1850, seemed most determinedly radical. If anything, the increasing prominence of the 'New Germans', Liszt and Wagner, strengthened his own commitment to Classical ideals, and it was those ideals which, if they kept the bitterness out of his actual music, can also make that music seem in some respects a retreat from the radical iconoclasm of his earlier works. When *L'enfance du Christ* (completed in 1854) actually achieved a·success – 'so great as to be positively insulting to my earlier works' – the composer sought to refute those critics who felt that the oratorio marked a complete change in manner and style with the retort that 'the subject lent itself to a mild and simple kind of music'. And he proceeded to state his artistic credo, directed against 'the mass of the Paris public': 'To such people all music that deviates from the narrow path where the makers of *opéras-comiques* toil and spin inevitably seems and has seemed for a quarter of a century the music of a lunatic. To them Beethoven's supreme masterpiece the

Ninth Symphony, and his colossal piano sonatas, are still the music of a lunatic . . . For myself, I am a free-thinker in music, or rather I am of the faith of Beethoven, Weber, Gluck and Spontini, who believe and preach, and prove by their works, that everything is "right" or "wrong" according to the effect produced, and that this is the sole criterion for condemning or exonerating any given arrangement of notes.'

After this, it might seem scarcely surprising that it was not until the twentieth century – the great age of 'free thinking' in music – that justice was done to Berlioz. Before that could happen, criticism had to move to the opposite extreme from that of the kind quoted earlier – Schumann, Verdi – which characterized him as a disconcerting iconoclast and eccentric. According to Debussy, for example, 'Berlioz was never a musician of the theatre. There is real beauty in *Les troyens*, a lyrical tragedy in two parts; but owing to its defects of proportion it is difficult to perform and the effect produced is monotonous, not to say tedious . . . Besides, Berlioz put nothing

16 An especially extravagant page from the manuscript score of Berlioz's *Grande messe des morts* (1837), showing the entry of the four brass groups in the Dies Irae. Also shown in the centre of the page, the large percussion section.

original into it. It is reminiscent of Gluck, whom he passionately loved, and Meyerbeer, whom he cordially detested. No, that is not where Berlioz is to be found.' Debussy of course, exaggerates. *Les troyens* may not be revolutionary for the late 1850s, and the early acts may be slow-moving, but it seems extraordinary that Debussy should have been deaf to Berlioz's unsurpassed gifts as a melodist, and to the personal quality and expressive distinction of such episodes as Hylas's song, or the great love duet.

Even less acceptable today is Debussy's gibe that Berlioz was always anxious 'to prop up his music with literature' – not because the literary connection is not crucial, but because Berlioz made of it something so original, so ambitious, so forward-looking; and only if both *Roméo et Juliette* and *La damnation de Faust* are dismissed as second-rate or worse can one sustain the argument that on this count alone Berlioz was a failure. Even if the three purely instrumental symphonies are deemed too trite to take seriously, *Benvenuto Cellini* too congested, the *Grande messe des morts* too bombastic (or simply too

17 Caricature by Gustave Doré of Berlioz conducting the chorus of the Société Philharmonique, which he founded in 1850. It lasted little more than a year.

dull), *L'enfance du Christ* more saccharine than sober, and the two late operas simply too retrograde for comfort, those remarkable products of the period between 1839 and 1846 cannot be easily ignored. If they are indeed 'hybrids', they are hybrids of startling power and substance – superbly Romantic gestures of challenge to formal convention in opera and symphony alike.

In both categories, Berlioz's radicalism seems most evident in his resistance to that increasing organicism commonly seen as central to the development of musical Romanticism. Thus *Roméo et Juliette* does not merely multiply sectional subdivisions within its four parts, but seems to take delight in exploiting contrast for dramatic effect, and even as devout a Berliozian as Hugh Macdonald has accepted that in this work 'the term symphony has been stretched to breaking point' as a result of 'Berlioz's fondness for juxtaposing seemingly incongruous elements in a composite work . . . the deliberate result of his striving to match every subject to its ideal expressive means'. The most fundamental juxtaposition in the work is that between the vocal and instrumental episodes, for it is a consequence of the essentially narrative role of the vocal sections that there can be little in the way of expansive melodic writing (the Air for Friar Laurence in the finale is one of the least memorable sections). The absence of distinctive vocal melody is contrasted with the richly characterized material of the main orchestral movements, most powerfully of all in the 'Scène d'amour'. From a twentieth-century perspective, *Roméo et Juliette* can be seen as a strikingly imaginative expansion of the fundamental symphonic design, rather than an outright destruction of that design, and an anticipation of the kind of 'Modernist' mosaic structures which are the logical consequence of the abandonment of tonality.

The more familiar we become with juxtaposition and super-imposition as formal devices in modern music, the less disconcerting we are likely to find Berlioz's strategies – though they remain impressively forceful and confident for their time. These qualities are even more evident in *La damnation de Faust*, that 'légende dramatique' that was once an 'opéra de concert'. Here there is a more consistent use of text than in *Roméo*, and the discontinuities in the treatment of the story are more cinematic than surrealist; even if the four principal parts seem in outline to be built up from a piling together of intentionally disparate episodes, Berlioz composes some superb musical transitions to connect those episodes – for example, that

18 Portrait by Courbet of Berlioz in 1860: the period of *Les troyens* and his greatest disillusionment with French musical life.

between Mephistopheles's *Song of the Flea* and the *Chorus of Gnomes and Sylphs* in Part II. *Faust* is also notably rich in its confirmation of Berlioz's mastery of orchestration and of the fact that for him 'melody is the most vital agent of musical expression' (see p. 64 above); there are magnificent melodies for widely contrasted moods, from the delicate dance of the Will-o'-the-Wisp to the wistful 'chanson gothique' for Marguérite, *Le roi de Thule*, to Mephistopheles's exuberant Serenade – as surely 'a caprice written with the point of a needle' as anything in *Béatrice et Bénédict* (to which Berlioz's remark applies).

Those who particularly admire the radical Berlioz of *Roméo* and *Faust* may occasionally admit to disappointment that he did not follow up these fascinating if flawed experiments. Berlioz himself was in no doubt that the major occupation of his later years, *Les troyens*, was 'a great work, greater than anything done hitherto'; and he added 'it seems to me to have an imposing grandeur and an extreme variety of moods'. The many judgments made on the work before 1969 must be assessed in the light of the fact that it was only in that year – the centenary of the composer's death – that the opera received its 'first wholly complete stage performance', in Glasgow. Today, a verdict like Debussy's only seems possible on the basis of ignorance or prejudice, or both, for even if *Les troyens* is in part the direct result of Berlioz's disenchantment with developments in contemporary music, it is much more than a mere rearguard action – anti-Scribe, anti-Wagner. Stimulated, at least initially, by contacts in Weimar with Liszt's mistress, Princess Sayn-Wittgenstein, it powerfully counters the prevailing orthodoxy of French grand opera, described earlier: that need to 'contribute to the Romantic activity of criticizing current social evils and proposing improvements' (see above, p. 59). Berlioz offered – as did Wagner – a reinvigorated mythology, though without Wagner's concern for contemporary relevance, and underlining his personal lack of interest in transcendental issues of philosophy and religion. It was admiration for Gluck and Virgil, rather than enthusiasm for certain contemporary political and social thinkers which stimulated Berlioz, and when he wrote of an aria from *Iphigénie en Tauride*, 'whose colour of antiquity, solemnity of accent, and desolate dignity of expression in melody and accompaniment recall the sublimities of Homer and the simple grandeur of the heroic age, while filling the heart with the unfathomable sadness inseparable from the memory of a glorious but vanished past', he was identifying those preoccupations of his own which found fulfilment in *Les troyens*.

These comments also show how an essentially Romantic character, the conjunction of 'simple grandeur' and 'unfathomable sadness', could be expressed through 'melody and accompaniment'. Simply because *Les troyens* does not embrace the progressiveness of Wagnerian symphonic–motivic processes, while tackling a mythological subject, it can either seem to fall between the two worlds of Wagner and Verdi – or else to bridge the gap, triumphantly, between them. That rare phenomenon, the music-lover who rates Verdi and Wagner equal first in the nineteenth-century operatic pantheon, is likely to see Berlioz as failing to match either the dramatic flair of the former or the sheer musical power of the latter. By contrast, 'pure' Verdians may prefer Berlioz to Wagner – more melodic, less pretentious – while 'pure' Wagnerians may also prefer Berlioz to Verdi – more serious, more substantial. One way or another, therefore, the long-delayed discovery of the 'true' *Troyens* has vindicated Berlioz's faith in his own ideals and techniques, and there are certainly few today who would argue that anything by

Meyerbeer, much by Donizetti – and even, possibly, anything by Verdi before his late masterpieces – can surpass it.

It is scarcely surprising that after his concentrated work on *Les troyens* Berlioz should have felt the need for what he called a 'relaxation', in the form of *Béatrice et Bénédict*. With this *opéra comique* he seemed to set the seal on his highly individual anti-progressiveness, and – as has often been pointed out – the work is as felicitous a demonstration of a composer's ability to find melodic equivalents for the rhythms and cadences of his native language as Verdi's final comedy, *Falstaff*. In his essay on the *Symphonie fantastique*, Schumann wrote of Berlioz's melodies stripping off their peculiarities to 'reveal a more universal and loftier beauty', and it is this ultimate simplicity of melodic character that strengthens the sense of Classical background to Berlioz's Romanticism. It is the fusion of a personal tone with a very simple shape that makes Berlioz's finest melodies so distinguished. Of course, he was by no means the only Romantic composer to make melodic expressiveness the central element of a style whose vitality and individuality were more than a match for the Classical achievements of previous generations. Yet he shares with the greatest of his fellow-Romantics the ability to invent appropriate contexts for his melodies – textures, harmonies, forms – and it is because the totality of the result is so distinctive and absorbing that Berlioz's own greatness is, ultimately, beyond challenge.

CHAPTER SIX

'The scent of Paradise':
Chopin's radicalism and the imagery of Romanticism

When Chopin (1810–49) first met the novelist George Sand, in the autumn of 1836, he had already enjoyed five years of remarkable success in Paris. Chopin and Sand became lovers in 1838, and it was in April 1839 that Sand wrote to a friend that 'this Chopin is an angel; his kindness, tenderness and patience sometimes worry me, for I get the idea that his whole being is too delicate, too exquisite and too perfect to exist long in our coarse and heavy earthly life. At Majorca, when sick unto death, he composed music full of the scent of Paradise; but I am so used to seeing him away in the skies that it does not seem to signify whether he is alive or dead. He does not really know on what planet he is living and has no precise notion of life as we others conceive it and live it.'

It would be difficult to imagine a more Romantic description of a great Romantic artist, or an interpretation more determinedly oriented towards an emphasis on a composer's contact with the sublime – with Hoffmann's 'spirit realm'. Yet the twentieth-century mind will need little convincing that there is more to Chopin's compositions of the period 1836–9 – including the completion of the op. 25 Etudes and Trois nouvelles études, the op. 33 and op. 41 Mazurkas, the F major Ballade, the C sharp minor Scherzo and the Sonata in B flat minor – than the 'scent of Paradise', just as Sand's claim that he had 'no precise notion of life as we others conceive it and live it' seems a sentimental extravagance in the light of the picture that emerges from his own letters. As a composer, Chopin was both the purest of the early Romantics in his concentration on keyboard music and its smaller forms (even if we choose to interpret that concentration as involving a fascinating and radical rethinking of 'smaller' forms in the light of other composers' larger structures), and the most obvious 'outsider' in a Romantic world whose grosser manifestations he detested. Although in 1833 he could boast that 'I enjoy the friendship and esteem of the other musicians' in Paris, he had as little enthusiasm for the music of the other major Romantics as they had true appreciation of his. He certainly admired the way in which Liszt played his (Chopin's) compositions, but had little sympathy with what he saw as Liszt's excessively mannered and flamboyant creations.

Such judgments are scarcely to be wondered at in view of the fact that Chopin's own background was so different. And while it is easy to exaggerate the special circumstances of his early years in Poland, as well as the ironies of his rapid and sustained success in a city where Berlioz, for one, could find little but frustration and incomprehension, it may well be true that it was a mixture of detachment (by virtue of his birth) and confidence (by virtue of his success) that did most to enable Chopin to pursue such a remarkable policy of transcending the superficiality and easy effects of the salon piece in his years in France. He was also fortunate in that, disinclined by temperament to engage in the barnstorming platform antics of the concert virtuoso, he was able (after 1832) to avoid frequent concert appearances through the patronage of, among others, the Rothschild family. Indeed, he gave only about thirty public performances throughout his life. Nevertheless, his life was not exclusively devoted to creative work, sheltered by the protection of his patrons. He was in demand as a teacher, and in his last years, at a time of social upheaval in Paris, he found himself experiencing the harsher side of patronage in travels through England and Scotland. It was in these final, bitter months that he may have come closest to regretting that he had never accepted the challenge of his teacher Elsner, expressed in a letter to Chopin of September 1834, not merely to compose an opera on a subject drawn from Polish national history, but to return from his 'Olympian abode' in Paris to his true homeland. It is true that as a composer Chopin had as little interest in detailed programmatic pictorialism as he had in large-scale dramatic or symphonic forms. And as a 'nationalist' in exile he was inclined by temperament more to allusion to Polish features as an aid to refinement of expression than, as later nationalists would be, to affirmation as a means of intensifying emotion and originality – through partial but significant independence of French or German models.

Chopin was virtually self-taught as a pianist, and as a composer his lifelong concentration on the piano was established early – a draft for one of his best mazurkas (op. 7 no. 4) has been assigned to 1824, when he was only fourteen. His first piano lesson and first publication (a G minor polonaise) date from his eighth year (1817), his first public performance from a year later. And although it was not until 1826 that Chopin began full-time music study with Elsner, he was already showing a lively interest in contemporary music: a letter to a friend of June 1826 shows that he had been studying the score of *Der Freischütz* in advance of a possible Warsaw performance, and he noted ruefully that 'considering the aim that Weber had in mind in his *Freischütz*, its Germanic substance, its queer romanticism, its extraordinarily *recherché* harmony (which particularly suits the German taste) one may reckon that the Warsaw public, accustomed to Rossini's light melodies, will begin by praising it not from conviction, but rather in imitation of the *connoisseurs*, and because Weber is highly thought of everywhere'.

While it is not difficult to read into this wry portrait of relative provincialism the strength of Chopin's desire to escape into a wider musical world, he was no more contemptuous of (or uninfluenced by) Rossini's 'light melodies' than he was by Weber's '*recherché* harmony'. Yet the fullest musical embodiment of that essential 'elegance' that Chopin himself was to do more than any other composer to establish as a serious feature in music of genuine substance was Hummel, who visited Warsaw in 1828, and whom Chopin set out to emulate. It is primarily because of the sources of Chopin's style – Hummel, Field, Weber, Rossini, Bellini, Spohr (rather than Beethoven or Schubert) – that he might be seen as, in some sense, evading the challenge of the larger-scale symphonic sonata. Even if it could be established that in the late 1820s it was possible for him to be fully aware of the achievements of the Viennese masters, however, it would be more sensible to regard his independence of, or indifference to, the potential of their work as recognition both of where his own gifts lay and of what music needed in the 1830s: that is, time to digest those great works of the late Classic era before seeking to develop their implications. And that 'digestion' could well involve the kind of smaller-scale but highly imaginative adaptation of sonata-form characteristics that several of Chopin's finest works reveal.

When Chopin paid his first visit to Vienna in 1829 his concern was certainly not with a city recently deprived of two towering geniuses, but with the recognition there that 'I am a virtuoso of the first rank, to be counted in with Moscheles, Herz and Kalkbrenner.' However,

74

19 Chopin's early virtuosity. Manuscript of the opening of the Variations on 'Là ci darem la mano' from Mozart's *Don Giovanni* (1827).

back in Warsaw, in October 1829, he reported that 'I've never heard anything so great' as 'Beethoven's last Trio . . . In it Beethoven snaps his fingers at the whole world.' Perhaps this was the main lesson Chopin learned from Beethoven: that a composer confident of his own genius can afford to snap his fingers at the world, even if he does so in a very different way from Beethoven's when it comes to matters of style and form.

Chopin's early successes in Poland were great enough to make it clear that he could best fulfil his talents and further his career by travel to the grander centres of music: and it was to Paris, not Vienna, that he committed himself. In September 1831, at the age of twenty-one, he arrived in the French capital: 'I reached Paris quite safely although it cost me a lot, and I am delighted with what I have found. I have the finest musicians and opera in the world . . . You find here the greatest splendour, the greatest filthiness, the greatest virtue and the greatest vice.' His first concert, in February 1832, when he played the E minor Concerto and the op. 2 Variations, ensured his success, and it is a credit to the Rothschilds, the Stockhausens and other patrons that they recognized Chopin's special quality: that he was not just another showman. Many testified to his qualities as a performer: in 1835,

Mendelssohn reported that 'there is something fundamentally personal and at the same time so very masterly in his playing that he may be called a really perfect virtuoso' – even more importantly, he was 'a proper musician'. A year later, Schumann, who became a critic of Chopin-the-composer's failure to rise to the challenge of the German Classical legacy, reported that, besides the G minor Ballade, 'he played a whole number of new studies, Nocturnes and Mazurkas – everything incomparably. It fills you with emotion merely to see him sitting at the piano.' Then, with an understandable lack of objectivity, Schumann declared that 'Clara is a greater virtuoso and plays his compositions with even more significance than he does himself.'

As for the actual significance of the compositions, Schumann's reservations are well-known. As already noted (p. 37), while he considered Chopin the finest of the many pianist–composers based in Paris, he regretted the fact that his highly personal musical style seemed not to have developed over the years. What Schumann failed to observe was that, far from developing by expansion, Chopin intensified expressiveness and refined structures to such effect that the results can now be seen as laying the foundations for that new flexible coherence of form in all genres which is the hallmark of Romantic music after 1850. The leading proponent of this 'alternative symphonism' in Chopin, Gerald Abraham, claims that, as early as the Mazurka op. 24 no. 4 (1834–5), he began to expand and refine simple sectional forms, so that with another Mazurka, op. 41 no. 1 (1838–9), 'we already reach the almost symphonic style of the greatest Mazurkas of the last phase'. This symphonism consists in increasing or introducing thematic development in forms – waltz, nocturne, polonaise – more normally associated with the simple statement and restatement of contrasting thematic elements.

Even if it is felt that there are dangers, in using the terms 'symphonic' and 'developmental', of exaggerating the nature of these compositions as in some sense offshoots of the Classical tradition, it is perfectly true that their most remarkable quality is sophistication of compositional technique in all its aspects: not just a more elaborate thematic working, but more varied phrase structures and richer harmonies (extending diatonic tonality) than mere dance forms would normally be expected to display. In 1830, long before the composition of the most radical works of his later years, Chopin wrote from Vienna about the public popularity of waltzes by Strauss and Lanner: his own mazurkas, he points out, 'are not meant for dancing'. A decade later, it was the mazurkas, as 'serious' compositions, which were to provide the basis for the powerful extension of their thematic, phrase-structural and harmonic techniques into later and larger works. In the 1830s only the G minor and F major Ballades and the B flat minor Sonata anticipate – not entirely successfully – that greater scope and power which emerge fully in Chopin's compositions after 1841. The later mazurkas (including op. 68 no. 4, Chopin's last composition) intensify still further the chromatic enrichment of their basic tonalities, and developmental processes grow even more pervasive. But it is in the third and fourth Ballades (1841–2), the E major Scherzo (1842), the F minor Fantaisie (1841) and the Polonaise–Fantaisie (1846) that Chopin's radical approach to form – building new structures from the elements of the old – can best be demonstrated, in works whose greater expressive power reflects the conviction and originality of their techniques. These works do indeed evoke a 'Paradise' of personal freedom – an utterly individual response to a recognition of the need to make form serve the new expressiveness without lapsing into incoherence.

As Gerald Abraham suggests, it is the Polonaise–Fantaisie which is the most exceptional for Chopin in its radical reshaping of ternary or sonata-type models, yet completely successful in the way its relatively free succession of events is balanced and controlled by reference to one, central tonality of A flat major. And although the piece may be felt to anticipate the kind of structures found in Strauss's symphonic poems at the end of the century, its immediate significance, in the mid-1840s, is as a pointer to the increasingly confident independence of Classical models, in both symphonic and operatic music, which was to emerge after 1850, in music which Chopin himself might well have regarded as the height of coarseness and crudity.

Of course, Chopin the man was by no means merely the delicate sophisticate of popular myth. He could be pungent in thought and word, as his letters show, and his finest works are not only subtle in mood, but strong in form. That strength, as in the Polonaise–Fantaisie, may not be inconsistent with a sense of the improvisatory: we should never forget the contemporary evidence that 'Chopin *never* played his own compositions twice alike, but

20 Portrait by Delacroix of Chopin in 1838, the year of his first visit to Majorca with George Sand, and of work on some of his finest keyboard works, including the op.28 *Préludes*.

varied each according to the mood of the moment, a mood that charmed by its very waywardness'. Even if this does not mean that he literally added ornamentation to melodies, or reduced or extended passages on the spur of the moment, his art is clearly the enemy of the four-square and the unspontaneous. And this emphasizes the fact that his music has a particularly intimate connection with the technical characteristics of the type of instrument for which it was composed. The early-nineteenth-century piano, its hammers covered with layers of felt or soft leather, was, with its soft tone, ideal for this purpose, and no other composer, not even Liszt, made such poetic use of its potential.

Understandably, few historians can resist the conjunction between Chopin's death and the changes in Europe after the 1848 revolutions. Chopin's final appearance on a concert platform in Paris was in February 1848. That same month, the citizen-king, Louis-Philippe, was deposed, and life in the city where Chopin had found 'the greatest splendour' and 'the greatest filthiness' changed for ever. Chopin himself spent most of 1848 in England and Scotland, and, weakened by years of illness, he expressed an accidie which confirms the sense of foreboding, of irreversible change. Writing to a friend, he declared that 'we are a couple of old *cembalos* on which time and circumstances have played out their miserable trills . . . The soundboard is perfect, only the strings have snapped and a few pegs have jumped out . . . I am writing this nonsense because nothing sensible comes into my head. I am vegetating and patiently waiting for the winter. I dream now of home, then of Rome; now of happiness, then of misery. No one plays now to my taste . . .' And, in the most poignant of all cries from the greatest keyboard composer of the time: 'All those with whom I was in most intimate harmony have died and left me. Even Ennike our best tuner has gone and drowned himself: and so I have not in the whole world a piano tuned to suit me.' Eventually, in November 1848, Chopin was able to make the journey back to Paris, but his health continued to deteriorate and he died there in October 1849.

If Chopin's death seems to mark with particular decisiveness the dividing line between the two principal phases of musical Romanticism, it is in no small part because his own later music so strikingly anticipates those features of formal flexibility, diversity of phrase structure and tonal expansion which were to develop so powerfully during the second half of the century. Of course, other composers active well before 1850 – Berlioz, Liszt, Wagner and Verdi among them – also contributed towards that evolution, and would continue to be involved in it. Moreover, of the earlier Romantics who, like Chopin, belong essentially to the first half of the century, Schumann also did much to determine future developments. When it comes to bridging the gap between Beethoven and Wagner, or Beethoven and Schubert on the one hand and Brahms and Dvořák on the other, Berlioz and Schumann are indeed more convincing intermediaries than Chopin. (And while conducting this roll call, we should not forget Donizetti's importance as a bridge-builder between Rossini and Verdi.)

Yet simply to state the matter in this way is to underline that, in essence, no 'bridge-builders' were really needed between the Classical masters and later nineteenth-century symphonists and opera composers. Those later composers were quite capable of making their own connections and drawing their own conclusions. The earlier Romantic masters are to be valued in their own right: whether, like Berlioz, they remained committed to a highly personal projection of Classical ideals; whether, like Schumann, they came to believe passionately in the need to preserve and extend the traditions established by Beethoven; or whether, like Chopin, they were able, by both temperament and technique, to prove that a major contribution to the evolution of music was possible without any particular interest in symphony or opera – or in Classical ideals. Chopin's relative lack of concern with the Classical heritage does not make him any more purely Romantic than the others, of course, for Romanticism – an extraordinary mixture of creative selfconsciousness and spontaneous expressive intensity – is as heterogeneous as it is distinctive. The great Romantics after 1850 were also to contribute mightily to that heterogeneity, that distinctiveness. And it was, perhaps, only after their contributions were complete that it became possible for music-lovers (and historians) to do justice to the achievements of their precursors.

CHAPTER SEVEN

Liszt and Wagner: the high Romantic drama

In an essay written in 1911, the year of some of his own most radical, and instinctive, compositions, Schoenberg described, rather tortuously, what he saw as the central paradox of Liszt's life and work: the failure to harmonize conscious and instinctive forces. Liszt (1811–86) 'consciously replaced the old form by a new, and the old visionary form by a third party's vision, instead of his own. These two acts of his consciousness prevented the discovery made by his intuition from being transformed directly and purely into an artistic deed ... Thus he produced second-hand poetry instead of exclusively allowing his own visionary form, the poet in himself, direct musical expression.'

Schoenberg is at his loftiest in this essay. He mentions none of Liszt's symphonic poems by name – and only one other work, the oratorio *Christus*. Yet his feelings come most fully into focus – as do those of many other writers on Liszt – by means of a comparison with Wagner. 'Although his [Liszt's] work ... seems to fall a little short of certain demands, one must not overlook how much there is in it that is truly new musically, discovered by genuine intuition. Was he not after all one of those who started the battle against tonality, both through themes which point to no absolutely definite tonal centre, and through many harmonic details whose musical exploitation has been looked after by his successors? Altogether his effect has perhaps been greater, through the many stimuli he left behind for his successors, than Wagner's has been – Wagner, who provided a work too perfect for anyone coming later to be able to add anything to it.'

Whether or not this statement is literally true – and it is, perhaps, truer with regard to Liszt than Wagner – it expounds in appropriately extravagant terms the idea that Liszt was less successful than Wagner in realizing his vision of a new musical form dedicated to expressive, poetic, dramatic themes and subjects. The great nineteenth-century anti-Wagnerian, Eduard Hanslick, was also scathing of what he saw as Liszt's failings as a composer, though he was full of praise for Liszt the pianist: 'His playing was free, poetic, replete with imaginative shadings, and, at the same time, characterized by noble, artistic repose . . . What a remarkable man!' As a composer Liszt failed to satisfy Hanslick's main demand, that music should be based on its own laws, 'thus making, even without a programme, a clear, independent impression. The main objection to be raised against Liszt is that he imposes a much bigger – and abusive – mission on the subjects of his symphonies: namely, either to fill the gap left by the absence of musical content or to justify the atrociousness of such content as there is.'

For Hanslick, it was an even greater heresy to attempt to transform the symphony into a programmatic drama than it was to try to transform opera into something radically new. For Hugo Wolf, by contrast, Liszt's radical intent demanded respect, and even admiration: 'Liszt's music . . . is more intelligent than deeply felt, but vividly and warmly fanciful, and always plastic . . . Liszt strikes us as being by nature no more the absolute musician than Berlioz. What Liszt has over Berlioz is that with the utmost security he has created a new form in the sense that he willingly gave priority to the poetic idea, then, in order to develop the idea artistically, had to depart, inevitably, from the traditional symphonic form . . . He had to let the musical form be determined by the substance of the poetic outline.' And in his obituary notice, Wolf argued that 'intelligence, depth of thought and feeling, and an incomparable sense of beauty in musical forms are the characteristic distinguishing features of his creations. In this respect, the symphonic poems, including *Faust* and the *Dante* Symphony, stand out above all the rest. The whole romantic enchantment of Liszt's demonic personality pours out to us in these compositions. They are his most personal works.'

The contrasting views of Hanslick and Wolf on Wagner and Liszt are familiar. A century later, Hanslick's view of Wagner is generally seen as historically interesting rather than critically convincing. With Liszt, however, Hanslick's point remains acute: and doubts about his true stature as a composer persist. Of all the great figures of Romantic music, it was Liszt who most directly linked the age of Beethoven to the age of Schoenberg, writing a Diabelli variation at the start of his career (1822) and music which verges on atonality at the end. But it usually seems safest to characterize him as the nineteenth-century composer with the longest career, rather than the greatest

21 Wagner looming over Liszt's shoulder. A silhouette said to represent Liszt playing Beethoven's *Hammerklavier* Sonata.

achievements. What cannot be questioned is that Liszt, like Wagner, was a great Romantic: in the range of his compositions and the various phases of his life he exemplified all that is most thorough-going and consistent in musical Romanticism.

Liszt could not claim a wholly inexplicable source for his musical gifts: his father, an official in the service of the Eszterházy family, was a good, and versatile, amateur musician. Yet there was something almost miraculous in the sheer rapidity with which Liszt was translated from obscurity (and poverty) to fame and fortune. Only a little more than two years separated his first public concert at Sopron (in October 1820, the month of his ninth birthday) and his first public concert in Vienna, on 1 December 1822. Within two years he was the rage of Paris, and it was in Paris that Liszt became wholly of his time, susceptible to the richest mix of diverse Romantic influences – literary, religious, sexual. Liszt shared the prevailing dislike in Parisian artistic circles of King Louis-Philippe, but, like Chopin, he profited from the more liberal atmosphere in French culture which followed the 1830 revolution, and for which Chateaubriand's doom-laden hero René was an emblematic figure. No doubt there was much that was superficial and meretricious in such a culture, where radical spirits sought patronage, and patrons regarded 'radicals' as sources of temporary and preferably undemanding excitement. That Liszt – again like Chopin – failed to fall in line as just another pedlar of virtuosic trivia cannot be ascribed simply to a superior keyboard

83

22 Portrait by Lehmann of Liszt in 1839, the beginning of the period when he reached the height of his fame as a travelling virtuoso.

technique or greater than average musical sensitivity. There was an evident conflict of ideals within him – or a conflict of ideals and instincts – of the kind that is difficult for the historian to reconstruct without creating an atmosphere of pure melodrama, but which must be described because it provides a background to the other great tensions of Liszt's life – between performance and composition, and also between the France that formed him and the Germany that stimulated and challenged him in later years.

As early as 1827, the year of his father's death, Liszt, in a phase of nervous strain, had formed the wish to become a priest. Then, as his career as a virtuoso developed, and alongside his first love affairs, he grew interested both in Saint-Simonism and in the teachings of the Abbé Félicité de Lamennais. Liszt spent the summer of 1834 in retreat with Lamennais at his country estate, and the experience seems to have prompted a marked advance towards maturity in the piano compositions sketched there, which included *Apparitions* and the *Harmonies poétiques et religieuses*. It is hardly surprising that Liszt should have been attracted to Lamennais's views about the divine status of art and the priestly function of the artist. To the sceptical, historically-knowing mind of a later century, there is something both naive and ironic about the idyllic summer at La Chênaie, so short a time before Liszt's elopement to Switzerland with Marie d'Agoult. Yet such contrasts and dramas were not just evidence of Liszt's determination to live life to the full. As would happen in later years with Liszt's daughter Cosima and son-in-law Richard Wagner, the creative ideals of the composer – however priestly in purpose – were held to require precisely the kind of sacrifice with respect to convention and convenience that the relationship in question inflicted on all concerned. Now that the successful creative artist was, socially, free to follow his own high ideals, it was inevitable that these would conflict with the orthodoxies of societies whose own attitudes had not, correspondingly, changed.

There were three main strands to Liszt's long and complex life, all subject in various ways to the conflicts and tensions described above. First, his personal, sexual and family life, dominated by the relationships with Marie d'Agoult, from whom he finally separated in 1844, and Princess Carolyne Sayn-Wittgenstein, whom he met on tour in Kiev in 1847, and whose attempts to secure a divorce over the next twelve years were doomed to failure: her husband did not die until 1864, and she and Liszt never married. (A full account of this aspect of Liszt's life would also consider his relationships with other women, as well as with his children and their spouses – notably Wagner.) The second strand was that of the professional performer: the pianist and conductor. Here the main division is between the period dominated by piano playing and composition, 1835–47, when Liszt, having virtually invented the piano recital as we know it today, travelled Europe from London to Constantinople, and the years in which conducting was his principal activity. Liszt was actually offered his post in Weimar in 1842, although he did not commit himself to it full-time until 1848, and it was from that year onwards that the most celebrated events of his directorship occurred: for example, the performances of *Tannhäuser* and Part III of Schumann's *Scenes from Faust* in 1849, the première of *Lohengrin* in 1850, and the Berlioz weeks of 1852 and 1855. Liszt's championship of other composers' – often difficult – music can now be seen as one of the most creditable aspects of his long career; yet, as a nineteenth-century Grand Ducal Director of Music Extraordinary, even he was subject not just to the prejudices of critics but also to the whims of the aristocracy. By 1859 his position in Weimar (and, even more so, the position of Princess Carolyne) had become very difficult, and although he never completely severed his connections with the city, they were much less close after 1861.

The third strand of Liszt's life, and the most important in the present context, was as a composer – though naturally this cannot be completely separated from his activities as a performer, especially from the concert-giving that new developments in the design of the piano promoted. Many historians have written at length about the Parisian spectacle of contests between virtuosi, and of the commercial rivalry of the piano makers Erard and Pleyel, whose workshops produced a remarkable and rapidly changing variety of domestic instruments aimed at the new and fast increasing middle-class market. However, pianos which were perfectly adequate for the domestic market could not always stand up to the demands of the great virtuosi. String-snapping was a frequent occurrence before the 1860s, when the much stronger instruments of Steinway and Bechstein emerged, and Liszt would often have two pianos on the platform and move between them during his recitals. As for Liszt's virtual invention of the solo recital, this can be illustrated by his concert at the Hanover Square Rooms in London on 9 June 1840, when, for the price of 10s 6d, or 21s for a reserved seat near the piano, the audience could hear a programme including several arrangements or transcriptions (the Scherzo and Finale from Beethoven's *Pastoral* Symphony, the *Serenade* and *Ave Maria* by Schubert), and three of Liszt's own pieces: *Hexaméron*, *Tarantelles napolitaines* (from *Venezia e Napoli*) and *Grand galop chromatique*. Liszt has often been accused of making little effort to improve public taste on these occasions. Yet whatever the content of one typical recital programme may have been, the catalogue which Liszt himself compiled of the works he played in public between 1838 and 1848 is eloquent testimony to his discrimination as well as his versatility and virtuosity: for example, it includes all the later Beethoven sonatas.

For many historians and critics, Liszt's sheer productivity as a composer, coupled with the prominence of transcriptions and paraphrases of other men's music, has served to reinforce suspicions that he could not possibly have been either very serious or very discriminating in his creative work: the contrast with such dedicated souls as Berlioz, Wagner or Brahms seems extreme. At best, it might be inferred, Liszt was akin to Verdi in that he rose well above the routine without radically transforming existing conventions: though, unlike Verdi, his final works were less the apotheosis of their genre in their time than an anticipation of very different times and techniques to come. It may well be that Liszt never wholly outgrew, or wished to outgrow, an approach to composition laid down as early as 1824, in such trifles as the *Impromptu brillant sur des thèmes de Rossini et Spontini*, and the *Allegro* and *Rondo di bravura*. Even so, his fascination with the diabolical skills of Paganini (the first fruits of which were a *Grand fantasie sur La clochette de Paganini* in 1832) and his relish of the challenge of transcribing the whole of Berlioz's *Symphonie fantastique* for piano in 1833, were balanced, even in those relatively early years, by his feeling for the capacity of the piano to perform the more 'priestly' function of expressing vision and mystery, as well as of enhancing expression through a focus on the poetic, the programmatic, rather than on the pure abstractions of Classical tradition.

The works written during the summer months spent at La Chênaie in 1834 have already been mentioned, and it is the harnessing of pianism, whether virtuosic or not, to serve more intense and durable expressive ends which, more than anything else, helps to ensure that Liszt is still taken seriously as a composer. Just how progressive and withdrawn from virtuoso flamboyance such expression could be is exemplified in the short piano piece *Il penseroso* (planned in 1839), a work of economical intensity whose chromaticism (though still controlled by fundamental tonal forces) matches the visionary nature of the subject – a statue by Michelangelo – without incongruity or overstatement. Progressive in harmony yet simple in structure, *Il penseroso* is an archetypal Romantic composition. Yet, like Schumann (and unlike Chopin), Liszt may have come to believe that, while it might in theory be both more radical and more Romantic to avoid large-scale forms altogether, the kind of subject-matter and modes of expression to which he felt drawn demanded a greater time-scale, a grander canvas. And, again like Schumann, his devotion to Beethoven – fuelled by the inside knowledge gained from having begun to transcribe the symphonies for piano during the 1830s – did not discourage him from attempting larger (if not exactly comparable) forms.

It was nevertheless only gradually, during his Weimar years, that Liszt came to the composition of larger-scale, and relatively 'abstract', works: the two piano concertos, the Piano Sonata (1852–3), the series of twelve symphonic poems (beginning with *Ce qu'on entend sur la montagne* in 1848 and ending with *Hamlet* in 1858; a thirteenth, *Von der Wiege bis zum Grabe – From the Cradle to the Grave –* was composed in 1881–2), the *Faust* Symphony (1854; chorus added 1857) and the *Dante* Symphony (1855–6), as well as the bigger choral works. By the late 1840s, Liszt was well established in Weimar, and the resources available there encouraged him to attempt more ambitious compositional schemes.

Yet several of the major projects completed by Liszt in Weimar – including the two symphonies and the *Dante* Sonata – had been conceived long before, in the late 1830s. Indeed, the sense of fulfilment at this time is all the greater for the feeling that long-meditated possibilities were being successfully realized. There is probably little point in seeking to make absolute stylistic or structural distinctions between the predominantly programmatic works and those with titles like concerto or sonata: nor can it be claimed that a single-movement or conflated sonata scheme is by some magic process inevitably superior – more subtly unified – than a scheme with three or four quite separate movements. Yet what impresses about Liszt's Piano Sonata in B minor is precisely the sense of structural innovation serving expressive intensity. Because there is a single movement embracing elements – first movement, slow movement, finale – normally kept separate in Classical sonatas, the composer ensures overall cohesion of structure and enhances the great diversity of mood by carefully controlled harmonic processes and easily recognizable, regularly recurring thematic cells. To enhance cohesion while expanding form seems as fundamental a Romantic ambition as to enhance refinement and intimacy by concentrating form, and much consideration has been given by musicologists to the possibility that these apparently 'expanded' forms are in effect sequences of miniatures run together. Certainly, it is in the nature of Romantic 'synthesis' to allow for a good deal of flexibility in the order and relation of the component parts. Yet Liszt's best one-movement forms, like the acts of Wagner's music dramas, cannot seriously be regarded as direct ancestors of twentieth-century 'indeterminate' or 'moment' forms, where the order of events can change from performance to performance, and interchangeability is built into the composer's basic conception. Liszt's ability – especially evident in the Piano Sonata – was to construct a thrilling tonal and thematic drama by challenging, but ultimately confirming, the most essential characteristics of goal-directed symphonic organization: and it is not in the least surprising that he should have sought to discover the kind of poetic subjects for his symphonic poems that would enable comparable structural means to be employed.

There are plentiful antecedents for Liszt's symphonic poems in his various single-movement treatments of poetic subjects in the larger pieces of the *Années de pèlerinage* for piano, like *Vallée d'Obermann* and *Après une lecture de Dante*. Apart from Liszt's own earlier work, the antecedents lay in those various symphonies and concert overtures that professed either a generalized poetic 'tone' (Beethoven's *Pastoral*) or a programme susceptible of quite detailed development (Berlioz's *Fantastique*). From Mendelssohn's *A Midsummer Night's Dream* Overture to Berlioz's *Lear*, from Schumann's *Manfred* to Wagner's *Faust*, the appeal of demonstrating music's Romantic skill for the magical, wordless transformation of poetic text and character into atmosphere – into pure expression – was irresistible. Liszt's own search for suitably Romantic imagery is most notable, perhaps, in *Orpheus*, *Prometheus* and *Hamlet*, this last described by the composer as 'an exceptional person' who 'imperiously demands the wine of life and will not content himself with buttermilk'. Hamlet's attitude to Ophelia is that of the typically wilful, solitary Romantic artist: 'He wishes to be understood by her without the obligation to explain himself to her . . . She collapses under her mission, because she is incapable of loving him in the way he must be loved.'

Though they are now thought of exclusively as independent concert works, many of the tone poems were first conceived as parts of other pieces or as overtures for plays, or other compositions. If such origins suggest a degree of indecisiveness on Liszt's part as to their true nature, one may also detect degrees of doubt as to how best to organize their structures. The series is undeniably a testimony to Liszt's weaknesses as well as to his strengths, and anyone engaging on a chronological sampling may well be disheartened by the repetitious and episodic character (as well as the thematic banality) of no. 1, *Ce qu'on entend sur la montagne* (after a poem by Victor Hugo). Nor does Romantic music come much more vulgar, or pointlessly protracted, than in *Hungaria* (no. 9), and although the more restrained and economical *Orpheus* (no. 4) despite its curiously salon-like material in places, and the intense, *Tristan*-like *Hamlet* (no. 10) have found particular favour with critics seeking continuity with Liszt's more visionary miniatures, both earlier (*Il penseroso*) and later (*La lugubre gondola*), the best music in the symphonic poems is not that of brooding tragedy but of harnessed and directed energy: for example, the post-Beethovenian briskness of parts of *Tasso* (no. 2) and the whole of *Festklänge* (no. 7); moreover, for all their heated rhetoric, the same quality can be found in *Héroïde funèbre* (no. 8) and even, to a degree, in the repetitive but never static *Hunnenschlacht* (no. 11). Ironic though it may be, therefore, it is Liszt the heir of Beethoven – even though he never matches Beethoven's ideal balance of scale and power – rather than Liszt the contemporary of Berlioz and Wagner, or the precursor of Strauss and Schoenberg, who produces the most memorable music in these tone poems. Ample associations with Wagner and other Romantics from Weber and Schumann to Bruckner can certainly be heard, however, and not just in march-like, fanfare-based episodes: both *Die Ideale* (no. 12) and the second part of the *Dante* Symphony suggest the world of *Parsifal*'s Good Friday. Even in the late *Von der Wiege bis zum Grabe* the spirit of Beethoven is still briefly evoked – allied, intriguingly, to that of Brahms: and there are hints of *Parsifal* here too. As for the best and most personal Liszt, then the popularity of *Les préludes* (no. 3) is certainly justified to the extent that, for all its repetitiousness, it lacks the laboured transitions and ramshackle continuity of the least successful pieces.

Liszt's devotion to the tone poem did not lead him to renounce all interest in the poetic, programmatic symphony, and for many musicians it is the *Faust* Symphony, dedicated to Berlioz, who had introduced Liszt to Goethe's poem in the early 1830s, and whose *La damnation de Faust* so impressed him, that is Liszt's masterpiece. For Hugo Wolf, writing in the year of Liszt's death, the *Faust* Symphony was decisively and significantly superior to Berlioz's work. In *La damnation de Faust*, according to Wolf, 'Berlioz failed to achieve an organic work of art, congruent in terms of form and substance, such as the two compositions by Wagner [*Faust* Overture] and Liszt. His [Berlioz's] *Faust* is a fragmentary mosaic, a haphazard structure replete with the most beautiful details, but without a clearly conscious aim.' In one sense, certainly, Liszt's symphony is more organic than

Berlioz's dramatic legend, since the three movements are bound together by a relatively small repertory of thematic ideas representing the three characters – Faust, Gretchen, Mephistopheles – and with much cross-referencing between the movements. Nevertheless, it is difficult not to feel that Liszt was better at the art of thematic transformation than he was at the art of transition. As Bruckner was soon to demonstrate triumphantly, symphonic form can remain viably coherent and organic even if, within large-scale single movements, there are very clear divisions between the constituent sections. The problem with the first movement of the *Faust* Symphony is less the divisions between sections than the laboured way Liszt attempts to bridge the gaps. This, coupled with the short-breathed nature of his actual ideas, makes the movement seem overlong and lacking, not so much in organic interconnectedness, as in dynamic thrust towards an inevitable goal. The central 'Gretchen' movement, containing less extreme contrasts, is more successful in devising a suitably proportioned form for its material. And although the finale – 'Mephistopheles' – contains a dangerous amount of repetition and unvaried phrase-structure, the final chorus (which Liszt added later) crowns the work with music of genuine breadth – aided by elemental Wagnerian fanfares which bring an air of imposing inevitability to the proceedings.

The *Faust* Symphony may fail to match the Piano Sonata and the best of the tone poems in the conviction of its form, while also lacking that compression of structural elements which would underlie Liszt's finest later achievements. Yet it is easy to see why Hugo Wolf, whose ideal was to integrate poetic content with organic form – whether in opera or symphonic music – could regard Wagner and Liszt as complementary in their concentration on the two distinct genres. The significance of Liszt's large-scale orchestral compositions – and the *Faust* Symphony in particular – as an influence on Wagner in the 1850s is often, and rightly, cited. It is surely undeniable that what Liszt learned from Wagner was more crucial than what Wagner learned from Liszt; Wagner was certainly encouraged by Liszt's bold approach to harmony to intensify his use of chromaticism and dissonance, whereas what Liszt learned from Wagner was the possibility of organizing his music on a larger, more symphonic scale, and orchestrating more effectively. His later, large-scale works like *Christus* (1855–67) and *St Elisabeth* (1857–62) are the direct result of

23 Liszt conducting the première of his oratorio *St Elisabeth* in Budapest, August 1865.

these lessons. The problem is that these later large-scale works, however professional, do not show Liszt at his very best.

There can be no doubt that – after the Weimar years, at any rate – Liszt was more impressive (and has been far more influential) for experimental concentration than for large-scale organic synthesis. And nowhere was he more obviously un-Wagnerian than in his failure to complete an opera, a form which never ceased to fascinate him. He had written a very early one-act stage work, *Don Sanche* (1824–5), but although there are many sketches for a *Sardanapale*, and various other projects were mooted, nothing came of them. (The oratorio *St Elisabeth* was actually staged, at Weimar in 1881, but Liszt sensibly boycotted the affair.) Historians occasionally assume that it was Wagner's achievements which did most to inhibit Liszt (and others), but it also seems probable that Liszt's musical character simply did not lend itself to the kind of 'concreteness' that great opera needs. Quite simply, his sense of drama in music was different from

Wagner's, and it was perhaps more authentically Romantic, after all, to deal in the allusions and metaphors of instrumental programme music than in the three-dimensional characters and situations required in opera, or even oratorio. It was not through any inability to achieve musical continuity on a large scale in a vocal medium. However, continuity in itself is not enough: neither *Christus* nor *St Elisabeth* rises consistently above the level of efficiency and competence, and *Christus*, in particular, Schoenberg's admiration notwithstanding, is very uneven in quality.

For the best of the later Liszt, it is necessary to forget Wagner's example as a form-builder and concentrate instead on the fulfilment of Liszt's own propensity to achieve a high degree of stylistic individuality and expressive intensity through the exploration of radical harmonic structures and relationships – to turn Romanticism towards Expressionism, and tonality towards atonality. His finest late piano works remain, on the whole, faithful to Romantic poetic imagery – the three *Villa d'Este* pieces from the third volume of the *Années de pèlerinage*, the third *Mephisto Waltz*, *La lugubre gondola* 1 and 2, and *Am Grabe Richard Wagners*. The conjunction of Faust and Wagner in these compositions is, inevitably, striking, and in both cases Liszt is equal to the need to do the images full musical justice. Yet his late experimentation, so palpably evident in the unresolved discords and veiled (or even suspended) tonalities of these pieces, was nevertheless not confined to programmatic piano music, but reached into vocal music in a manner decisively different from the dramatic priorities of opera or oratorio. Liszt's religious life progressed to the point where, in 1865, he received the tonsure and the three subsequent minor orders. His most remarkable sacred composition is *Via Crucis – The Stations of the Cross* – for soloists, chorus and organ, begun in 1876 and completed three years later. Liszt may have had a conscious desire to create a new kind of church music, but what is most striking about *Via Crucis* is not the conjunction of well-established liturgy and experimental harmony, but the way in which this harmony convincingly expresses a rapt devotion, sounding more 'Impressionistic' than Romantic, and pointing the way towards musical developments very different from those most closely related to post-Wagnerian trends in opera and symphonic music. By the mid-1870s Liszt had not only freed himself from any such close relation to the dramatic aims and structural procedures of Wagner. He had even, perhaps, also begun to sense the radical possibility that 'fragmentary mosaics' and 'haphazard structures' of the kind Wolf found – and condemned – in Berlioz, might provide an imaginative and appealing route to the music of the future.

In discussions of Wagner (1813–83), the burning issue is rarely whether or not he was a greater composer than Liszt, but rather whether – in a kind of response to his own greatness – he simply went too far. In 1875 this was certainly Verdi's view: 'Wagner surpasses every composer in his rich variety of instrumental colour, but in form and style he went too far. At the outset he successfully avoided mundane subject-matter, but he later strayed from his idealistic aims by carrying his theories to extremes.' Verdi's view was not simply (like Hanslick's) that Wagner was at his finest in his earlier Romantic operas. More than twenty years later, near the turn of the century, he remarked that 'I never cease to explore Wagner's sublime world of ideas . . . The work which arouses my greatest admiration is *Tristan*. This gigantic structure fills me time and again with astonishment and awe, and I still cannot quite comprehend that it was conceived and written by a human being . . . The second act . . . is one of the finest creations that has ever issued from a human mind.' There may be a touch of wily Verdian irony in the tone of these remarks, but it was rare even for Wagner's opponents to condemn his work outright. Hanslick, who in 1846 had declared that 'Richard Wagner is, I am convinced, the greatest dramatic talent among all contemporary composers', and who objected to the fact that the later music dramas lacked the 'comprehensible melody, the alternation of dialogue with ensembles, choruses and finales' of the earlier Romantic operas, never sought to deny his 'born genius' – only the ends to which that genius was applied.

As for such devotees as Hugo Wolf, to them Wagner was not only a great genius: he exposed the limitations of all other, earlier Romantic composers; 'Wagner, certainly, had absorbed all the elements of romanticism, but what with the romantics was superficial and empty is sublimated by Wagner to symbolic profundity, to plastic images founded on exceptional human interest.' Implicit here is a refutation of Hanslick's argument that, from *Lohengrin* onwards, what Wagner's dramas lacked was 'real characters, persons of flesh and blood, whose fate is determined by their own passions and

94

24 Drawing of Wagner made by E. B. Kietz during the Paris years (1839–42), the period of the completion of *Rienzi*, the composition of *Der fliegende Holländer*, and acute financial difficulties.

decisions'. In Hanslick's trenchant phrase, 'a person who "must" is no hero of a drama, for he is not of our kind'. For Wolf, by contrast, 'human interest' was only the starting point for the images of 'symbolic profundity', whose psychological, spiritual resonances were so powerful precisely because the merely human was so definitively transcended.

Since Eduard Hanslick (1825–1904) is often portrayed as a dimwitted hack journalist, out of touch with the temper of the times to the extent of believing that beauty in music had everything to do with form and nothing to do with expression, it should be stressed that his book, *On Musical Beauty* (1854), is by no means an unyielding defence of the argument that music is, by its very nature, inexpressive. Hanslick certainly believed that music should be, as structure, an end in itself, rather than the mere servant of dramatic or poetic expression. Yet music still possessed the ability to represent feelings, metaphorically rather than literally – and in this sense Hanslick's thought would seem not totally at odds with that of Arthur Schopenhauer, for whom the glory of music was in its emotional depth, however untranslatable into mundane verbal equivalents, and in its status as a true copy of that instinctive, all-embracing 'Will' that contrasts with mere phenomena, or 'representations'.

Wagner's determination to grapple with such elusive philosophical issues indicates his concern to place music on the highest pedestal, and is one of the qualities that make him so different a creative personality from Liszt. Yet if Wagner was the stronger creative force, it may have been in part because, at bottom, he felt less easy in the world. Successful and widely admired as a conductor, he was not a virtuoso performer (although his skills as a singing actor were, reportedly, remarkable). He was a failure in Paris while Liszt was lionized there: and his eventual establishment at Bayreuth, while it may appear domestically more orthodox and stable – more bourgeois – than anything Liszt would have enjoyed, was more near to the world than firmly placed within it. It may be the ultimate irony that Wagner came closer to turning art into religion than the Abbé Liszt – if only by adopting a more radical attitude to the role of religion in art. Of course, Wagner's mature works add up to a much more coherent and comprehensive 'statement' than do Liszt's. The latter's powerful poetic sensibility (even when it produced music technically more progressive than anything in Wagner) is dwarfed by the philosophical resonances (elusive though their meaning often is) in Wagner's great music dramas, works in which means and ends alike are no less rich in content for the often raw dramatic power they possess in the theatre.

Whether or not we accept the view of Carl Dahlhaus that Wagner is best categorized as a Neoromantic – that is, a Romantic in an un-Romantic age, an age dominated by positivism and realism (features which, in Dahlhaus's view, had in general little effect on music between 1850 and 1900) – it is difficult not to feel, with Wolf, that the essence of Wagner's greatness lies in the degree to which he transcends, in emotional range and formal scope, the truly Romantic world of his immediate predecessors. And the more musicology reveals of Wagner's debts to his precursors and contemporaries, the more we learn of the trials and errors of his creative processes, the more remarkable and individual that greatness appears. Much effort has been expended by historians (especially since the horrors of the Third Reich, which sought to give the composer the kind of official status as racial cultural hero which, in his own lifetime, he would surely have accepted as nothing less than his due) to establish a 'demythologized' Wagner, and to determine the 'truth' about both life and works, identifying the falsehoods, prevarications, inaccuracies and fantasies of much earlier biographical and technical writing. The best of such work is, again, likely to increase admiration for the real achievement, even if it also intensifies regret at the all too human failings. As an artist, Wagner had the courage of his convictions, even if also, as a nineteenth-century bourgeois German, he had the incentive and the propensity to indulge all sorts of ancillary prejudices and eccentricities. To use the convictions to excuse the prejudices is no more acceptable than to use the prejudices to belittle the convictions. We may be thankful that, given everything else, the works themselves were so fine – though for some even that view is not possible. But in attempting to define what it is about the works that makes them fine, we also need to provide some context – a brief general account of Wagner's life and thought.

All biographies of Wagner begin with a question: was his father Carl Friedrich Wagner or Ludwig Geyer? It is unlikely that the answer will ever be known, although the fact that Geyer was a professional painter and actor, while C. F. Wagner (a police actuary) was only an amateur actor, casts the psychological weight in favour of Geyer. Wagner's early years were not as unorthodox as he later liked to suggest: in particular, his musical studies were more serious and extensive than he wished to admit in his autobiography. Nevertheless, there was an undoubted flair for things theatrical in early youth, and a certain inevitability about the progression from the wildly immature tragedy *Leubald* (1828) through to the sketches for an opera, *Die Hochzeit*, only four years later, and the execution of both text and music for his first completed stage work *Die Feen* immediately after (1832–4): though this was not performed in Wagner's lifetime. In 1833, at the age of twenty, Wagner became chorus master at the theatre in Würzburg, and his fifty-year career as a practical man of the theatre was launched. He had already appeared as a conductor of his own music, with the Concert Overture in C (Leipzig 1832), and his Symphony in C had been performed in Prague.

Returning from Würzburg to Leipzig at the beginning of 1834, Wagner made his first contacts with progressive intellectual circles (the 'Young Germans') and wrote his first published essay, *German*

Opera. Though by no means wholeheartedly radical in the (later) Marxist or Anarchist sense, the prevailing ideas in these circles involved a search for more forceful, less sentimental forms of artistic expression. They were already in revolt against the early Romanticism of, for example, Hoffmann and Weber, but they did not adopt a narrowly nationalistic view of what the sources of new forms of expression should be. It certainly suited Wagner to look beyond Germany for the elements of his own operatic style: only much later would he seek to reinforce a more purely Germanic provenance for his most radical and personal mature idiom, and this would happen only after his extra-musical activities obliged him to experience life in other countries at first hand.

Between 1834 and 1839 Wagner emerged as a promising, potentially front-rank opera composer and music director. Having left his post in Riga and lived in Paris from 1839 to 1842, he returned to Germany for the triumphant première of *Rienzi* in Dresden (October 1842), and the following year obtained a permanent post at the Saxon court in that city. By now, at the age of thirty (and with his stormy marriage to Minna Planer seven years old), Wagner had already completed (in Paris) another, much more forward-looking opera, *Der fliegende Holländer* (first performed in Dresden in January 1843), and had begun to sketch *Tannhäuser*. His experiences in Paris had been traumatic (his financial position precarious in the extreme) but also artistically revelatory, through contacts with Meyerbeer and Berlioz, Scribe and Heine. Inasmuch as *Der fliegende Holländer* is an expression of Wagner in Paris, it is a declaration of his belief in his own superiority. It is also an intensely personal work which has far fewer links with the style of grand opera than does *Rienzi*; and while it may not be a greater work than Berlioz's *Roméo et Juliette* (first performed late in 1839) it could scarcely be more different from that 'dramatic symphony' in either technique or style.

The Dresden years, from 1843 to 1849, were intensely active and productive. Not only were ideas for all the later works beginning to ferment (a process helped by the library which he had begun to assemble) but Wagner was becoming increasingly critical of the artistic and political status quo. In 1848 he completed *Lohengrin*, produced his 'Plan for the Organization of a German National Theatre', and spoke and wrote about the relation of monarchy and republicanism: he also met the anarchist Bakunin. Various forms of discontent (including marital) served to fuel his restlessness, and when, in 1849, civil disorder reached Dresden, Wagner was inevitably involved. The nature of that involvement is a matter of dispute, but he was lucky to escape arrest, and was forced to flee, via Weimar (and Liszt), to Switzerland. His exile was to last twelve years.

Wagner's early development as an opera composer proceeded alongside his early activities as an opera conductor, and in neither case was he concerned only with German materials. Indeed, it is clear from his writing that he admired the work of French (or French-resident) composers – Gluck, Cherubini, Méhul and Spontini – as much as that of Beethoven, Weber, Spohr or Marschner. Increasingly, the musicological study of lesser-known figures serves to underline the truth that there is nothing new under the sun. For example, the following remark – 'If there were something to desire in this music, it would be a little more singing which would offer to spectators a bit of repose from multiple orchestral effects' – refers not to *Tristan* but to Cherubini's *Lodoïska*: it comes from the *Journal de Paris* of July 1791. And although the whole purpose of identifying such anticipations of Wagnerism (as of identifying the presence of reminiscence motifs or leitmotifs in the likes of Grétry and Méhul) is as much to point up differences as to establish similarities, those differences are themselves often more a matter of musical style than of basic technical principle. The exploration of such a style belongs to the prehistory of Romanticism, and cannot be pursued in detail here; yet it reinforces the point that the importance of Wagner lies less in what he literally invented than in what he did with what already existed – discovering potentials that no other composer, least of all among his immediate contemporaries in Germany, seemed able or willing to exploit.

It could nevertheless be argued that the most vital pre-Wagnerian development in opera was not the incidental or small-scale use of motivic recurrence, but the employment of networks of thematic correspondences and connections to promote larger-scale continuity, as the traditional separation of formal units in opera – recitative, aria, ensemble – was broken down. As we have seen earlier, German advances in this direction can be traced in Weber (*Euryanthe*), Spohr (*Faust* and *Jessonda*) and Marschner (notably *Hans Heiling*). It is usually claimed that it was the German association between expressive harmony and supernatural subject-matter which was more crucial than motivic practices as such in propelling Wagner to transform Romantic opera into music drama. But both features must have seemed to him ripe for the kind of broadening and intensification 'Young Germany' demanded. Wagner must have been as conscious of the deficiencies in the work of his predecessors, whether French or German, as he was of the merits. Moreover, in the mainstream of grand opera, as represented in the late 1820s and 1830s by Auber, Rossini, Meyerbeer and Halévy, the need to make the 'product' acceptable, and accessible, to the increasingly middle-class audience tended to result in vocal display and relatively 'realistic' subject-matter; yet despite the larger formal units introduced to underpin the elaborate stage effects and large ensembles (see Chapter Five above, p. 60), the possibilities of a more 'symphonic' thematic process remained unrealized.

There is, naturally, a danger of seeing Wagner's own early operas exclusively in terms of his response to 'historical' forces of which he may have had little conscious knowledge. Yet even without the exaggeration of a historian's hindsight the development those operas represent is strong and striking. *Die Feen* preserves a basic division of its acts into numbered sections, even though the presence of motifs used after the manner of Weber and Spohr can be detected, whereas *Das Liebesverbot* and *Rienzi* both make use of the large-scale, composite formal units which are a feature of Meyerbeer's grand operas, as Wagner himself noted in his essay (probably of 1840) about *Les Huguenots*. Even so, *Das Liebesverbot* and *Rienzi* would be of much less interest were it not also possible to detect Germanic melodic features too, however superficial. After all, Wagner's Paris years were important not just for contacts with Meyerbeer but for the indications of his developing awareness of the untapped dramatic resources in the music of Beethoven (and also, perhaps, of Berlioz) – resources of compositional technique involving symphonic thematic processes and increasingly integrated harmonic schemes as well as increasingly atmospheric orchestration. In these respects the *Faust* Overture (1840) is a work whose importance transcends its apparently peripheral status in Wagner's oeuvre.

Such resources were deployed most directly in an enriched harmonic vocabulary and a more subtle and varied orchestral palette, and it is possible to find plentiful evidence of such trends in German Romantic opera – Weber and Spohr, again – where techniques were certainly in advance of anything in France at the same time. As early as 1833 the theorist Antoine Reicha, in his *L'art du compositeur dramatique*, had suggested a direct link between new harmonic explorations and the sublime power of Greek drama. As indicated earlier in this chapter, however, it was the example of Liszt which Wagner himself – at least in retrospect – regarded as crucial: in a letter of 1859 he confessed that 'I have become a completely different fellow as a harmonist since my acquaintance with Liszt's compositions'. Yet the Wagnerian operatic revolution – the transformation of opera into music drama – could not be accomplished simply by increasing the amount of chromatic harmony or intensifying thematic cross-references. It was founded in deep, often obscure but potent cogitations on the nature of drama itself, and on the kind of subject and text that would, in Wagner's view, most decisively signal the rebirth of the medium.

That rebirth stemmed from the not inconsiderable achievement of Wagner's first three mature operas – *Der fliegende Holländer*, *Tannhäuser* and *Lohengrin*. Many would accept that these are the finest dramatic works of the 1840s, even when Donizetti's later works, Verdi's pre-*Rigoletto* operas, and Berlioz's *La damnation de Faust* are taken into account. The anguished central character of the Dutchman can easily be seen as a significant contribution to that procession of troubled heroes that stretches from *Rienzi* to *Parsifal*, and the vigour and directness of the music are irresistible. The more conventional elements of cadence, and even cadenza, are acceptable when the total effect is so firmly controlled and so clearly directed towards its goal – all the more strongly in the original one-act version, whose transitions foreshadow the total mastery of such processes in *Das Rheingold*. Even such well-tried features as the choruses that end Act I and begin Act II are thematically integrated with the rest of the work. And so it was not entirely inaccurate for Wagner, in 1864, to describe *Der fliegende Holländer* as an 'early, unassuming work which, for all that, is in my true style'.

So skilful is Wagner's characterization of the Dutchman himself – primarily by means of the relatively long Act I set-piece 'Die Frist ist um' – that the awkward abruptness of the opera's dénouement, with the Dutchman self-destructively eager to believe that his 'angel' is unfaithful, rather than clinging to the hope of 'redemption' for as long as possible, does little to weaken the work's impact. Such impulsiveness – the musical momentum sweeping past dramatic crudities – is turned to still more positive account in *Tannhäuser* and *Lohengrin*, in both of which the role of 'outsider' is again shown as anything but fulfilling and desirable. Both works are on a larger scale than *Holländer*, but in both there is a stronger sense of the elemental and the expansive, of basic ideas heard at the very outset which have all the immediate strength and far-reaching potential necessary to sustain dramatic life over long spans. The choral marches and ensembles of prayer and jubilation in both works probably do most to try audiences' patience today, but even these, when placed and experienced in context, contribute to the satisfying solidity of balanced diversities which is Wagner's real 'secret' as a form-builder. The Pilgrims' March music which begins *Tannhäuser* is a powerfully sustained, immediately gripping elaboration of a very simple theme, and other, very different episodes – Wolfram's Act II song, Tannhäuser's 'Rome' narration, the music for Ortrud and Telramund (*Lohengrin*, Act II) and Lohengrin's 'In fernem Land' – all have as a common factor this convincing directness and memorability.

It was not so much that Wagner was continuing the revisionist process of grand opera, eroding the old divisions of the 'number' opera and dealing with dramatic themes of greater immediacy: he was focusing on the need to balance formality with flexibility, and to show that the best way to sustain attention over long periods was to prepare climaxes and crises of maximum impact. The reduction of vocal display and (relative to Meyerbeer) of stage spectacle was balanced by richer harmony and orchestration. Even in these early operas the impression is created that these important, fundamental dramatic themes can be effectively handled in no other way. Well before the character of Klingsor was conceived, Wagner was showing that his greatness lay in his ability to enslave and elevate an audience. His opportunity to exploit that ability to the full was nevertheless delayed and frustrated for some years after 1849: until, in fact, the exile could return to found his own theatre and establish his own tradition.

Even if we take the 'Romantic' view that Wagner was in the grip of forces – the Fates? – who ensured that he lived his life with the sole purpose of making his work possible, we might concede that singularity of aim, and certainty of purpose, are more difficult to demonstrate than a succession of conflicts and contradictions, in which the disentangling of fact from fiction is as problematic as the separation of positive from negative. To take the year 1850 alone: the sketching of a section of *Siegfrieds Tod* (at this stage a single opera, but soon to become the fourth part of the *Ring* tetralogy) was positive in the sense that it showed Wagner determined to resume compositional activity after a break of two years, and negative in that the sketches served to reinforce his awareness of the chasm between his musical style and technique, on the one hand, and his dramatic ambitions on the other. The writing in 1850 of the essay *Jewishness in Music* could scarcely be claimed as other than wholly negative, were it not for the suspicion that the processes of thought it represented might have had an important part to play in the creation of the music dramas, with their evident belief in the opposition of superior and inferior orders, races, human types. Wagner's biography is so difficult to write not only because of the probable fictionalizing of events like the 'epiphany' of *Das Rheingold* at La Spezia, but also because the tracing of the interaction of life and works is always a matter for speculation, a minefield in which subjectivity can easily and destructively run riot. Even when what Wagner did can be established beyond reasonable doubt, the reasons why he did whatever it was may well remain unclear. And even when what Wagner actually wrote – for example in *Opera and Drama* – can be convincingly expounded, its actual significance remains a matter for debate.

As far as personal relationships are concerned, the later years of Wagner's life were in large part shaped by two factors – patrons and passions. Otto and Mathilde Wesendonck did most to make it possible for him to live and work in Switzerland in the 1850s, and had Minna Wagner died in 1854, when her heart condition took a turn for the worse, Wagner's love for Mathilde could well have developed more decisively than it did. In 1857, when this passion was at its height (and *Tristan* was being composed), Cosima and Hans von Bülow spent part of their honeymoon at the Wagners' house near Zurich. Wagner had first met Cosima Liszt in 1853, and much more time was to pass before this new passion matured; it was not until 1862 (after the traumatic experiences of the Paris *Tannhäuser*) that Minna and Wagner finally separated, and not until 1864 that the most passionate of all Wagner's patrons, Ludwig II of Bavaria, ascending the throne at the age of eighteen, made his melodramatic gesture of settling the Master's accumulated debts and inviting him to live in luxury near – and later in – Munich. It was then that Cosima joined Wagner, and

25 Photograph of Wagner in Paris, February or March 1860. Wagner was in France to conduct concerts and prepare the production of the revised *Tannhäuser*.

26 The Magic Fire Music – a page from Wagner's autograph full score of *Die Walküre* (Act III). This music, showing Wagner's orchestration at its most opulent, was completed in March 1856 when the composer was living in exile in Switzerland.

although Minna died in 1866 they were not able to marry until 1870, when Cosima's union with Bülow was finally dissolved.

The turbulence of life in Munich, from which Ludwig's devotion provided only partial protection, led to a further period of residence in Switzerland, and it was only after the choice of Bayreuth as the location for the Wagner Festival Theatre that Richard and Cosima settled into a permanent home – the specially built Wahnfried – in 1874. It was here that the *Ring* was completed (on 21 November), twenty-one months before its first complete performance in the new theatre (beginning on 13 August 1876).

Wagner's relationships with all who were close to him inevitably had their moments of tension – there was a violent argument with Cosima on the day of his death – and likewise many commentators on his work have uneasy responses, not so much to the music dramas, for all the debates that rage about how they are most properly interpreted and analysed, but to the prose works, and the nexus of ideas and attitudes they represent. Wagner wrote relatively little about music as such, but even the voluminous outpourings of the 1849–51 period (in the fields of aesthetics and autobiography) did not exhaust his desire to express himself in prose. In particular, once he was established in Bayreuth (the bulk of the full-scale autobiography dictated to Cosima, and the essay on Beethoven, were among the writings of the pre-Bayreuth, 1864–70, period) his status as a cultural 'guru' seemed to demand a series of pronouncements for the edification of his followers, one of whom – for a relatively short period – was Nietzsche. Such essays as *Public and Popularity*, *Religion and Art* and *Heroism and Christianity* are not merely reactionary but racialist, and opinion will no doubt be permanently divided as to the extent to which such effusions corrupt – or merely complement – the message of human perfectibility which lies at the heart of the last music drama, *Parsifal*. It would indeed be excessively extreme to argue that the literary evidence for Wagner's own extremism actually destroys his credibility as a great musical dramatist. The evidence should neither be suppressed, nor explained away by special pleading. But even when such evidence is given the fullest attention the music dramas stand as so powerful a demonstration of the positive force of human creativity (and for much more than the dubious ability to mesmerize and manipulate other humans) that whether we deem them the inevitable or paradoxical product of a mind like Wagner's, it is their greatness which most urgently demands attention. And Wagner's Romanticism may ultimately be seen to reside in the triumphant extraction of such power and positiveness from the extreme contrasts and contradictions both of his basic materials and of his own personality.

Wagner's greatness as a music dramatist lies in his treatment of epic subject-matter on an epic scale, with a consistently high level of imagination and conviction. There is (to all but the most unsympathetic listener) no sense of the trivial being inflated, or of matters that would be better dealt with pithily and economically being dragged out to unacceptable lengths. There are demands on the stamina of listeners and performers alike, of course, but it is less convincing to argue that, for example, Wotan's narration in Act II of *Die Walküre* is disproportionately long and dangerously thin in musical substance than it is to claim that this episode is a necessarily extended but absorbingly structured example of characterization serving a larger dramatic purpose. Wagner could control a rapid succession of events if he decided it was dramatically justified (notably, in what is admittedly the least typical of the music dramas, *Die Meistersinger*) but his technique was founded on the convincing interaction, and mutual stimulus, of the local and the large-scale, the miniature and the macroscopic: the large-scale is not so predetermined that all flexibility and tension are lost, and the small-scale is never so random or self-contained that its contribution to the whole is seriously called into question.

Wagner's 'revolution' is often said to involve new types of subject, a new style of text (stressing alliteration and variable line-length rather than end–rhyme and regular metres) and an appropriately new kind of music, with, as its central feature, the 'musico–poetic synthesis' – a particularly intimate and well-balanced fusion of verbal and melodic features that serve the drama directly, without constant reference to the conventions of traditional structural principles, regular (four-bar) phrases, or such closed forms as the aria, whether the da capo or cantabile–cabaletta variety. Put thus, the musico-poetic synthesis may sound indistinguishable from the driest recitative, and one can understand Berlioz's cry of protest in a letter of 1856 to Princess Sayn-Wittgenstein, complaining of Wagner's 'crime' – arguing, in *Opera and Drama*, that music should be 'subservient not just to drama but to text'. In practice, however, what most decisively transforms 'dry' recitative or declamation into Wagnerian arioso of an expressive force capable of sustaining the great weight of character and situation demanded of it is the presence of the orchestra, and the allocation to the instruments of significant dramatic material in the form of leitmotifs in particular harmonic contexts, not merely to illuminate the immediate moment, but to help control and determine the large-scale musical progress of drama from origin to goal. The musico-poetic synthesis is not, therefore, the entire act of creation, and in giving the blended word-melody a harmonic, tonal structural context of suitably flexible solidity, Wagner's genius is no less forcefully and originally at work. As is well known, one of Wagner's initial, theoretical intentions, announced in *Opera and Drama*, and arising out of his acute dissatisfaction with the state of the art in Germany, was to rescue text (and with it subject) from the slighting conventions of modern opera at its worst; and the first two parts of the *Ring* give the clearest indication of the 'ideal' realization of that theoretical intention, the verbal text in many places far from subordinate. Thereafter, whether through the influence of Schopenhauer, or simply as the inevitable result of music's nature, the pre-eminence of tone as the dramatic essence of music drama could not be denied, and Wagner's ability to invent memorably simple musical ideas and project and manipulate them on an unprecedentedly large scale came into its own. It is not that the texts are subjected to old-fashioned rhythmic distortions and formal conventions as a matter of course, but that the claims of musical form and process – even if less truly symphonic than the Beethovenian ideal made desirable – inevitably come into the forefront of the composer's mind. Wagner may be less 'careful' with his text after *Das Rheingold* and *Die Walküre*, but it says much for the sheer musical power of those works that the relative austerity of their texture in places cannot be convincingly analysed as a 'weakness'.

In recent years Wagner studies have been much concerned to promote a shift from discussion of links between text and theme (leitmotif) to one between subject and structure (harmony and tonality). To the extent that this involves a shift from the music's instantly audible foreground to its sensed but less explicitly experienced background it may seem primarily a matter for specialists. But its broader importance lies in the way it may serve to strengthen the impression of Wagner's historical significance as a great Romantic. Although he saw himself as Beethoven's heir, and the character of his materials and methods of organization are certainly not inconsistent with a strong debt to the master of dramatic development within the symphony, his music is also, to no small degree, an extension of the expressive and technical resources of earlier Romantics. In Wagner's hands the flexible miniature forms and allusive harmonic procedures of Schumann, Chopin and the earlier Liszt are not without 'influence' on the grandly proportioned designs of his dramas – even if the connection is more a matter of sensing things 'in the air' than of direct influence. In addition, the ambitious, technically progressive, if (at times) stylistically uncertain, poetic structures of Weber, Berlioz and the later Liszt undoubtedly encouraged him to pursue his own vision of music drama with the confidence of someone who knows that it is possible to do better.

27, 28 Setting by Max Brückner for Act III of Cosima Wagner's 1886 production of *Tristan* at Bayreuth. Its solid naturalism contrasts strongly with Wieland Wagner's design for the same scene (Bayreuth 1966).

Already in *Das Rheingold* the progression from a refreshing playfulness to a rhetorical grandeur (which some find overdone but which is surely psychologically and therefore dramatically right) shows a commanding range and originality which would stand as a summit and a challenge for the rest of the century and beyond. And what makes Wagner's saga-and-myth-derived subject-matter ideal for Romantic music drama is not so much such elements as the emphasis on nature or the supernatural as the portrayal of human vulnerability as itself an ennobling phenomenon: supremely so with Wotan and Hans Sachs (the more affectingly vulnerable because of their heroic stature) but also, perhaps even more impressively, with less sympathetic characters: with Siegfried telling the story of his life in a way that will ensure his death; with Amfortas fighting the weakness caused by weakness; with Isolde, at peace only in the awareness that she is passing beyond both love and life.

Even the exalted tone of fulfilment at the end of *Parsifal* is supremely Romantic in its dramatization of the Quest concluded: and in that conclusion the expansiveness is itself a celebration, more compelling than any brisker Classical peroration, of the human

agency, the divine served by man, and man exalted by the (passive) divinity. Hanslick's specific attack on *Parsifal*: 'In everyone involved there is wanting precisely that which makes for dramatic character: free self-determination in good or bad' – coupled with his more general complaint that 'Wagner's music affects the soul less than the nerves: it is not moving so much as eternally exciting' – vividly expresses the most honest contemporary doubt about where it might all end. Even if we regard the first remark as irrelevant and the second as understandable but, for most people in the post-Wagnerian era, untrue, we can still admire Hanslick's honesty as he adds: 'The most valuable and the most beautiful aspect of Wagner's activity is the sincerity and strength of his effort . . . With a rare fund of uncurbed energy he pursues the path which he is convinced is the only right one.' It is only a short step from this to Schoenberg's vision of Wagner's 'perfection' cited near the beginning of this chapter. Of course, that 'perfection' is unreal, but the sincerity and strength are not, and coupled with that 'uncurbed energy' they make Wagner the most formidable of all Romantic masters, both in his immediate effect and in his long-term challenge – and example – to posterity.

CHAPTER EIGHT

'Half vulture, half phoenix':
Verdi's Romantic synthesis

After the priestly, philosophical pretensions of Liszt and Wagner, Verdi's sheer robustness, his down-to-earth vigour and uninhibited relish for both vocal display and simple, heartfelt lyricism may seem a breath of fresh air. The no-nonsense full-bloodedness of Verdi may not invariably make the music of Chopin, Schumann, Berlioz or Wagner seem ultra-refined by comparison, of course, but it certainly points up the differences between the varieties of Romanticism displayed by those masters and one that, at least in its early stages, often avoided the banal only through the sheer bravado of its elemental forcefulness and verve.

In due course Verdi (1813–1901) was able to outdo both Bellini and Donizetti in musical substance as well as in animal vitality. Nevertheless, until the 1850s he was as much beholden as they to the dominance of the voice in Italian opera; the kind of musical enrichment achieved in France and Germany through descriptive orchestral writing was unknown. Also, Verdi's powerful sense of concentration and economy was at first scarcely compatible with the expression of those more reflective, lyrical facets of Romanticism so prominent in Germany and France. Verdi's forte was for Romantic melodrama, and his ability to extend and enrich a medium which, at its worst, displayed a seemingly bottomless capacity for blending the empty and the predictable, the crude and the improbable, depended on his developing both the desire and the capacity to dictate to singers, impresarios and librettists. To become more satisfying, and more sophisticated – as Donizetti also realized – Italian opera had to give more emphasis to dialogue, interaction, continuity. Arias must earn their place through relevance to the drama, and virtuosity must be a facet of character. Verdi was also to learn, though not until such middle-period works as *La traviata*, that melodrama is the more effective when contrasted with pure pathos, or with romantic love at its simplest and most poetic. Nevertheless, however strong Verdi's awareness of the artistic rightness of such factors, he could scarcely

29 Portrait of Verdi, *c.* 1843, painted about the time of the composer's great early success *Nabucco* (1842).

have set them in train had not the nature of his personality, and the circumstances of his life, made sustained and consistent progress beyond inherited conventions possible.

Verdi's life was very different from that of a typical eighteenth-century composer: and, in Italy, it was significantly different from that of earlier nineteenth-century ones. He achieved financial independence, progressing from the status of 'galley slave' to man of property, and in his later years he was able to choose his own collaborators and subjects; his later works were not simply commercial objects, but expressions of the man. Indeed, there seems to have been a particularly close relationship between Verdi's character, and certain events of his life, and his ability to bring a greater degree of humanity, and of dramatic conviction, to the elements of Italian melodrama than did his predecessors or contemporaries. And while such connections between life and works can be posited with most if not all great composers, the concreteness of those connections in Verdi's case lends them particular interest and significance.

Some of the decisive events in Verdi's life would have seemed more commonplace, if no less tragic, in his time than in our own. Others were by any standards exceptional, not least the early development and encouragement of his musical gifts despite his relatively unpropitious family circumstances – his father was an innkeeper in a small, provincial, north Italian town. He had his first success, as a conductor, in Milan, in 1834, at the age of twenty-one; five years later, in November 1839, his first opera, *Oberto*, was premièred in the same city, at La Scala. His career was launched – but in the circumstances of the greatest personal tragedy. In August 1838 and October 1839 he had lost the two children of his marriage to Margherita Barezzi, and in June 1840 (three months before the disastrous première of his second opera, the comedy *Un giorno di regno*) Margherita herself died.

The failure of *Un giorno di regno* was reversed in March 1842, with the première of *Nabucco*, a powerful portrait of a tyrant taught the error of his ways. There was certainly a political relevance to Italians in the theme of an enslaved nation achieving liberation. But *Nabucco* has musical virtues too, not least an approach to vocal characterization that transcends convention by sheer flamboyance, as well as a melodic breadth – evident in the famous chorus 'Va, pensiero' – that combines instant memorability with a strong sense of forward movement and large-scale formal control. The twelve operas that Verdi composed in the nine 'galley years' between *Nabucco* and *Rigoletto* (1851) made him the leading Italian composer, and his liking for subjects which were not merely based on stage plays of relatively recent vintage (like Victor Hugo's *Hernani*) but which also tackled subjects whose relevance to nationalist aspirations was not lost in Italy, offers an obvious and pertinent contrast to Wagner's development in Germany after *Rienzi*. Wagner's interest in politics was certainly not purely theoretical, but his aim seems to have been to change society in order to make it a fit recipient for true music drama, rather than to use opera as it then was to promote radical political causes. To Wagner, Verdi's efforts to bend librettists to his will might well have seemed like a futile attempt to disguise Verdi's own failure to take a sufficiently radical approach to the failings of contemporary opera: for all his success after *Nabucco*, Verdi seemed unable, in

Wagner's terms, to become a 'true' poet, and write his own texts.

But the contrasts between Verdi and Wagner do not end here. During the civil unrest of 1848–9 Wagner was driven into exile, while Verdi returned to Italy from Paris in August 1849, and his work had already played its part in reflecting the still-frustrated hopes of those who wished to free Italy from Austrian domination and achieve a united nation. From 1846, when the audience at a performance of *Ernani* in Bologna sang the praises of the newly elected Pope Pius IX to one of the opera's themes, to 1848, when the subject of *La battaglia di Legnano* ensured it a triumphant première in Rome, Verdi caught the mood of a people ready and willing to challenge the occupying power. Yet as hope turned into disillusionment – the Austrians would not be expelled until 1861 – so *La battaglia di Legnano* found less favour. Indeed, one might expect that the harsh events depicted in the opera which had preceded it – *Macbeth* (1847) – would have seemed more appropriate to the national mood after the failure of the 1848–9 revolt.

Of all Verdi's operas before *Rigoletto* it is *Macbeth* which seems – at least to the later twentieth century – to offer the clearest evidence of the composer's ambition as well as of his power and skill. It is a remarkable attempt to respond to one of Shakespeare's darkest

30 *The Battle of Legnano* (1860) by the Romantic Italian painter Amos Cassioli. Verdi's opera with the same title (1848) was initially a great success, but lost favour when it became clear that the occupying army of Austria was not to be driven out.

tragedies, whose lack of a love relationship was disturbing to many in the nineteenth century. Verdi's desire to tackle a theme with a fantastic, supernatural dimension was actually seen by some critics at the time of the opera's première in Florence to underline his inferiority to Mozart, Weber, and even Meyerbeer, although one anonymous notice used the comparison with Meyerbeer as a compliment: 'He [Verdi] has unfolded a genre which, until now, was not thought within his reach: it contains pieces which Meyerbeer would be pleased to have composed.'

Analysis of *Macbeth*'s relatively flexible form, and of its apparent concern for tonal structuring and symbolism, bears out the remarks of Verdi's contemporaries about his evident need 'to abandon the usual formulas'. Yet the undoubted advances of *Macbeth* were themselves soon to be surpassed. *Luisa Miller* (1849) demonstrates a distinct shift away from the hard-edged and forceful to a more delicate, intimate style, with a new emphasis on ways in which the orchestra can contribute to the drama. And then, after *Stiffelio* (1850), Verdi composed in remarkably rapid succession the three masterworks which form the bridge between his earlier and later manners – *Rigoletto* (1851), *Il trovatore* (1853) and *La traviata* (1853). These operas represent a startling advance in confidence and character, a development which it is difficult not to link with one of the most important events in Verdi's private life.

It was towards the end of 1847, when in Paris to prepare for the première of *Jérusalem* (an adaptation of *I Lombardi*) that Verdi fell in love with Giuseppina Strepponi, whom he had known since she sang Abigail – badly – in the première of *Nabucco* five years before. Strepponi was to become Verdi's closest companion, and although they did not marry until 1859, and the relationship had its inevitable moments of turbulence, she provided Verdi with invaluable support and sympathy until her death in 1897. Not even the happiness he found with Giuseppina was so all-consuming as to cancel out Verdi's habitual pessimism. But his liaison with her seems to have helped to promote his desire and ability, in the operas after *Macbeth*, to realize characters as individuals rather than stereotypes. And while Verdi's evident impulse to escape from cliché and convention, and to establish a type of music drama relevant to the time of its creation and revealing the full capacity of the human character, may not seem radically different from Wagner's, Wagner's own personal experiences in the 1850s – especially his association with Mathilde Wesendonck – seem to have led him in the opposite direction. Tristan and Isolde are more archetypes than individuals, and Wagner's concern with character does not imply any motion towards a more 'Realistic' brand of Romanticism. Verdi was far less interested in characters who gloried in being larger than life, and although it is a mistake to see *Rigoletto*, *La traviata*, or any of the later works as anticipating the *verismo* of Mascagni or Leoncavallo to any notable degree, the way in which his favourite dramatic topics, sexual love and family relations, are treated stresses his own concern to preserve the human dimension: to emphasize the vulnerable rather than the heroic. This, after all, was the personal preference of a man who never shared Wagner's belief in the need for the composer to claim and maintain a public position. Above all, Verdi valued his privacy.

One particular change of emphasis that is undeniable in Verdi's work (from *Luisa Miller* onwards) is away from subjects that treat the father–son relationship as supportive and constructive to a preference for subjects in which the father may be unsympathetic and remote. The biographical 'explanation' for this change may be found in the hostility of Verdi's own parents to his liaison with Strepponi, and possibly also in his sorrow at not being able to become a father himself again: after having had two illegitimate offspring and a miscarriage in the years before she met the composer, Giuseppina was apparently unable to bear more children. But here, for sure, such sources in the life (as distinct from the mind) for Verdi's creative preoccupations must be approached with special scepticism. For example, it is one of the most significant of all facts about Verdi that he 'failed' to compose a *King Lear*, and it seems perfectly plausible that he failed because, as he told Mascagni in 1896, 'the scene . . . on the heath terrified me'. Yet it is just as probable that *Lear* deterred Verdi because of its sheer intensity as through any links in his mind with the death of his own daughter. Speculation is, ultimately, futile: but it still helps to fill out our portrait of a composer who, for all his success, never ceased to question himself very searchingly about his work and how he could continue to perfect it.

Whatever the differences of opinion as to the relative merits of Verdi's earlier operas, critics and historians unite in regarding *Rigoletto* as his first major, and wholly mature, masterpiece. Many things combine to make it so – or rather, many things come into

31 Set design by G. and P. Bertoja for Act I Scene 2 of the first production of *Rigoletto*, Venice 1851. As usual in 19th-century stage design, the intention is to create atmosphere through essentially realistic representation.

purposeful and potent confrontation. Formal orthodoxy, used with maximum effectiveness, confronts new formal flexibility and integration, notably in Act III where, after the celebrated quartet, the urgency of the drama in its final stages overrides the possibility of breaks for applause between numbers. Comic and tragic, straightforward, four-square tunes and inspired lyric flights are all present, not in order to satisfy some theoretical equation of balance and symmetry, but to forward and enhance the drama. 'La donna è mobile' may seem to deserve its barrel-organ associations out of context, and likewise Rigoletto's displays of despair and grief may seem the stuff of meretricious tear-jerkers rather than high drama. Yet when experienced within the opera as a whole, contributing to its skilfully proportioned, brilliantly paced structure, such elements are not merely effective but perfectly suited to their purpose. In *Rigoletto* Verdi did not suddenly so far forget his Italian heritage as to decide to do things by halves, rather than whole-heartedly.

And should anyone suspect him of such timidity, they can turn to *Rigoletto*'s successor, *Il trovatore*, to redress the balance. As many recent authorities have claimed, it is unfair to *Il trovatore* to see it simply as a reversal to all the bad (or endearing) old habits of blood and thunder, toil and trouble. The work certainly does not build on the formal innovations of *Rigoletto*, but the dramatically pertinent contrasts between aristocratic, heightened lyricism and melodies of a rude vigour are no less significant here than in the earlier work. What sets *Il trovatore* apart in the company of *Rigoletto* and *La traviata* is its lack of a central character whose personality and motivation – 'psychology', to use an un-Romantic word – are modern enough to draw identifying emanations from the twentieth-century audience. Azucena is indeed a character with many points in common with Rigoletto, but she is, to put it mildly, 'larger than life': if she were not, *Il trovatore* would seem absurd rather than, for all its extravagance, compelling. Not surprisingly, however, critics who find in *La traviata* the first glimmerings both of that fascination with the low life of cities that fuels *verismo* and that restraint and acceptance of the value of understatement that proves Italian opera to be, at last, achieving greater sophistication, are also prone to see it as a reaction against that last fling in the direction of undiluted melodrama, *Il trovatore*. Yet *La traviata* can even more convincingly be regarded as the apotheosis of the early Romantic, bel canto tradition: and it gives what was often a rather thin connection between vocal melody and dramatic context a new intensity in the finely rounded portrait of the passionate, vulnerable, doomed heroine Violetta.

Like *Rigoletto*, *La traviata* conveys a strong feeling of tension between its moments of exuberance and its episodes of bitterness, its public and its private faces. It is an affecting work, and yet it is sometimes difficult for a modern audience to free its response to the opera's style and sequence of events from the silent-cinema histrionics it often seems to foreshadow. The music, while perfectly matched to the drama's shifts of atmosphere, is perhaps not sufficiently substantial to give the emotions themselves that timeless quality of the greatest art. It is no doubt a good deal more sensible to apply twentieth-century notions of psychology to the lives of nineteenth-century artists than it is to condemn their works for failing to display conscious recognition of the Theory of the Unconscious or the Oedipus Complex. But it may not be stretching the links between

Verdi's life and works too far to suggest that *La traviata* is perhaps too idealized – too anti-realistic – in its search for a lost innocence, its exposure of Violetta's fine feelings and heart of gold. The ending of *Rigoletto* is even more melodramatic than that of *La traviata*, yet in the earlier work the vital ingredients of bitterness and despair make the emotions that much more full-blooded and Romantic; and we are less likely to resent the composer's blatant appeal to our feelings in *Rigoletto* because the central character deserves our sympathy so much more than does Alfredo in *La traviata*. Both men 'get what they deserve': but whereas in *La traviata* we are more likely to mourn Violetta than to pity Alfredo, in *Rigoletto* our feelings are entirely with the survivor, the tragic father who has unwittingly contrived his daughter's death. This difference may help to explain the greater resonance and conviction of the earlier drama, and it also suggests that it was the theme of jealousy in family relations which brought out Verdi's truest greatness. As we would expect in a composer whose theatrical antennae were as sensitive as Verdi's, the musical differences between the two endings also reinforce the differences between the survivors: in *La traviata*, the music after Violetta's death is taut and to the point, but it scarcely crowns the drama with a statement of clinching significance. In *Rigoletto*, the protagonist's own last words (even though without motivic prompting in the music) underline with maximum economy the fulfilment of the curse on him with which the drama had begun. In true Romantic fashion, forces have been at work which are beyond the agency of mere humans.

Whatever one's final conclusions, if any, about such matters, the greatness of *Rigoletto* and *La traviata*, and their importance in the canon of Romantic opera, are difficult to overestimate. But such achievements often make difficulties for their creator, and it is occasionally argued that it was not until the completion of *Otello* more than thirty years after *La traviata*, in 1887, that Verdi produced an opera worthy to stand beside it. The harvest of this long period is a mere six works (not counting separately the adaptation of *Stiffelio* as *Aroldo* and the revisions of *Macbeth*, *Simon Boccanegra*, *La forza del destino* and *Don Carlos*): 'mere', because the period from 1839 to 1853 had produced no fewer than eighteen operas (excluding reworkings).

First, two years after *La traviata*, came *Les vêpres siciliennes* (1855), a grand opera written for a Paris to which, after 1850, such grandiose projects seemed increasingly passé. It certainly makes sense to see *Les vêpres* less as Verdi's carefully calculated response to what he felt Paris expected than as a deliberate attempt to do something new with the elements of a particular tradition, one widely regarded as moribund. For one great composer, at least, Verdi succeeded. Berlioz found in *Les vêpres siciliennes* 'a grandeur, a sovereign majesty more marked than in the composer's previous creations'. Later critics have on the whole been less positive, although they are likely to ascribe the work's shortcomings more to Scribe's libretto than to Verdi's music: even so, and for all its anticipations of Verdi's later manner, the grandeur in *Les vêpres* is not cumulatively convincing, the brief climactic violence almost risibly out of proportion and casually prepared.

Les vêpres siciliennes certainly did not exhaust Verdi's appetite for novelty. Indeed, its successor, the first version of *Simon Boccanegra* (1857), seemed so radical in its concentration, and its wide harmonic range, as well as its relatively plain vocal writing, that it met with general incomprehension. Nor, after the adaptation of *Stiffelio* as *Aroldo* (1857), was his next completely new work, *Un ballo in maschera* (1859), a consistent success at first, for although the première went well, it proved difficult thereafter to find three female singers of sufficient diversity yet comparable ability capable of doing it justice. *Ballo* is an intriguing work: the French associations – Offenbach and Delibes rather than Meyerbeer – are there, and, as if by way of compensation, the prospect of greater thematic interconnectedness, though scarcely of Wagnerian cast, is certainly in evidence. One twentieth-century Italian authority, Gabriele Baldini, has argued that *Ballo* is Verdi's greatest masterpiece, and while few may share that view many will acknowledge not merely that it triumphs dramatically over an unusual subject and a poor libretto, but that its purely musical strengths, of overall form and proportion, as well as the quality of individual ideas, are as fine as anything Verdi achieved between *La traviata* and *Aida*.

Un ballo in maschera is about the events surrounding the assassination of King Gustav III of Sweden, a plot which inevitably led to trouble with the Italian censors, and to versions which moved the action from Stockholm to Boston and Naples, with appropriate changes in the characters' names: the King becomes Riccardo, Count of Warwick in Boston, and Riccardo, Duke of Olivares in Naples. Part of the subject's attraction for Verdi was the opportunity it provided to pursue his Shakespearean desire to blend comedy and tragedy, and he does this in *Ballo* with greater subtlety than had been possible eight years earlier in *Rigoletto*. As well as an interaction between comic and tragic, there is an alternation of conservative and progressive procedures, the latter represented most powerfully by the large-scale duet for Riccardo and Amelia in Act II. The rarity of love duets in Verdi is often remarked on, yet in praising the undoubted intensity and strong emotion present in this example, it is important not to exaggerate its purely technical progressiveness. To put it bluntly, Verdi could have made the structure a good deal more 'Wagnerian' had he wished to, for example by fusing the end of the duet with the entrance of Amelia's husband (on the model of *Tristan* Act II, completed by Wagner in the same year as *Ballo*), instead of writing emphatic cadences which imply a break for applause. A genuinely Verdian progressiveness is evident in this duet in the way it builds on, and expands, the regular phraseology and relatively simple textures of the aria for Amelia which precedes it, thereby creating a continuity between the two episodes which goes beyond the mere smoothing out of cadences between their separate sections. In *Ballo*, and despite the notable importance of the orchestral contribution, composition for Verdi is still as much the art of juxtaposition as of transition – and even of superimposition, as the strong contrast of moods within the final ensemble of the act, with Amelia and her husband Renato on the one hand, and the two enemies of Riccardo on the other, makes clear.

In *La forza del destino* (1862), written for St Petersburg, Verdi continued to alleviate tragedy with comedy in another subject whose 'grand-operatic' qualities reveal little desire to follow up the intimate domesticities of *La traviata*. He also continued to make strong demands on his audiences: enthusiasts will indulge *Forza*'s richness, while sceptics are likely to find an unevenness that fails to justify the convoluted plot. Once more, however, unsolved problems seemed to make Verdi more determined to pursue possible solutions rather than to seek alternatives. His next opera, *Don Carlos*, composed for Paris and first performed in 1867, is certainly a less convoluted tale than *Forza*, but it is a work on the grand scale, and focused clearly on a subject dear to Verdi's heart, in which freedom for both individuals and nations is a necessary ideal, and the torments and isolation of one who wields great power are rendered with a direct but eloquent pathos that makes King Philip one of the supreme figures of Romantic opera. The work was heartily disliked by some, including Bizet, who declared that 'Verdi is no longer Italian. He is following Wagner.' This common complaint against the later Verdi no longer seems to make much sense, and even if in purely musical terms *Don Carlos* is uneven, it still displays a richness, freshness and balance of lyrical and dramatic elements sufficient to give the whole sustained conviction and intensity, despite its great length and despite the absence of contrasting comic episodes.

Comedy is also absent in *Aida* (1871). Here the most important contrast is between public spectacle and private emotion, a familiar Verdi feature, and while the ideal of 'freedom for both individuals and nations' is an obvious link with *Don Carlos* (not to mention several of the earlier operas) the sheer extravagance of the spectacle has left many musicologists uneasy. There is indeed a grand-operatic, even Meyerbeerian cut to the marching and countermarching of the triumph scene, and the musical riches apparent elsewhere may not compensate wholly for the naiveties of the libretto. The ceremonial march of grand opera certainly cast a long shadow over Verdi's work, and it is probable that those who can relish the symbiosis in *Aida* between such brash displays as the triumph scene and the tender exalted lyricism of 'O patria mia' and the final duet (recollections of Meyerbeer or not) are those who will be happiest with the work as a whole. Moreover, it may be precisely such enthusiasts – devotees of Verdi's unmediated conflicts between public spectacle and private emotion – who find the 'progressive' drift to greater, smoother continuity in *Otello* and *Falstaff* less convincing, if not actually a 'sell-out' to Wagnerism. That drift means, in practice, not only that arias and ensembles are more fully integrated into a continuous musical flow than formerly, but that the means of providing such integration – particularly the *parlante* (less speechlike than recitative, less purely melodic than aria) – itself gains greater prominence as the bearer of genuine musical substance. It was by this means that Verdi was at last able to achieve the necessary sophistication and integration of form to create the greater expressive intensity of his late operas.

The sixteen-year gulf between *Aida* and *Otello* (1887) was broken first by one of Verdi's greatest works, the Requiem, conceived in 1868 as a collective tribute to Rossini and then revived in 1873 as a personal tribute to Alexander Manzoni. That the music of the Requiem is not just dramatic but operatic is confirmed by the use of a discarded duet from *Don Carlos* as the basis for the 'Lacrimosa'. And in any case the glory of the work is that Verdi, far from self-consciously seeking to purge it of links with *La forza del destino*, *Don Carlos* or *Aida*, shows that the emotions of fear, awe, hope and resignation proper to the requiem text are indeed the generalized equivalents of those individual human passions so sharply drawn in the operas. Nevertheless, the glib judgment that the Requiem is Verdi's best opera ought to be reverently laid to rest: it is nothing of the kind, although it is probably the greatest of all requiems. And it also underlines Verdi's essential independence of the kind of influences, from France, Germany or anywhere else, that might significantly transform the style of his music.

The Requiem is a fine composition, not just an exhilarating, cathartic emotional experience, and it served to confirm Verdi's technical supremacy in the world of contemporary Italian music. Of course, the most striking parallel between German and Italian opera during the period after 1850 was precisely the dominance of single, supreme figures in each genre. Neither Verdi nor Wagner, even in their own time, was seen as merely *primus inter pares*: and to historians, the mouthpieces of posterity, both are so outstanding as to dwarf all their contemporaries in the field of opera into virtual insignificance. The musicological exploration of a particular period usually creates the impression that lesser figures are unjustly neglected, but even the most sympathetic studies of Verdi's Italian contemporaries can find little to enthuse over in the likes of Pacini, Faccio and the Ricci brothers, and not much more in Mercadante, Ponchielli and Boito. From Mercadante's *Il giuramento* (1837) to Boito's *Mefistofele* (1868) attempts were made at the kind of reform which could give dramatic conviction to a more elaborate musical substance than had previously been the norm, and which Verdi himself shunned. But the necessary masterpiece was not forthcoming. *Mefistofele* itself certainly has its moments – the beautiful duet 'Lontano, lontano, lontano', for example – but the moments fail to make a convincing whole. So, until Mascagni, Leoncavallo and Puccini began to make an impact, in the 1890s, the only Italian opera not by Verdi to generate much interest today is Ponchielli's *La gioconda* (1876).

During the three decades spanned by Mercadante's and Boito's abortive experiments, Wagner had single-handedly taken German

32 Lithograph of Verdi by Ape (Carlo Pellegrini), published in *Vanity Fair* (London, 1879).

opera from *Rienzi* (completed in 1840) to *Tristan und Isolde* (1859), *Die Meistersinger* (1867) and *Siegfried* (1871). And it is not surprising that, for a certain type of Wagner enthusiast, devoted to belief in progress, Verdi's actual achievement is a good deal less significant than the failure of Italy to produce a more exact equivalent to Wagner. After all, even if the failure of Italian progressiveness can be explained by such factors as the stringent censorship and the continued power and influence wielded by the most famous singers, a Wagner could surely have triumphed over such problems, as he did in Switzerland and Germany?

Seen from the standpoint of progressiveness, of radical reform, Verdi's achievement was certainly less spectacular than Wagner's. And yet, given the far stronger and more fixed operatic traditions he worked to transform, it is surely no less heroic, even allowing for the fact that its full fruition was due to the good fortune of a healthy old

123

age and an ideal collaborator (Boito) as librettist, whose own frustrated ambitions as a composer never for a moment soured the relationship. If Wagner was the Radical Romantic, Verdi was the Conservative Romantic – relatively speaking. But had Wagner been working from the basis of a tradition as well entrenched and vital as that of Italy, even he would probably have made far less rapid progress towards the Music of the Future.

The modern critical temper has little taste for the comparison of unlikes which must occur when Verdi and Wagner are placed side by side. The music lover who enjoys both and sees their complementary virtues is happy to have the best of both worlds. Yet it is probably difficult to be a wholehearted enthusiast for both. The devotee of Wagner's immense interlocking paragraphs will find Verdi's characteristic (and frequent) cadential emphases blatant, and evidence (even in the late works) of restricted perspectives. The devotee of Verdi's concentrated forms and deliberately extreme contrasts may find Wagner over-unified, his continuity more aimless than purposeful: Stravinsky, in *Poetics of Music*, has given the extreme statement of this attitude. Wagner was often (though not invariably) closer to that archetypal nineteenth-century concern with organicism, and more the anticipator of early twentieth-century techniques in his enriched harmony and complex motivic processes. But Verdi's early aesthetic is arguably more relevant today than it was in his own lifetime.

If he was not, then, a 'progressive', he embodied an approach to large-scale musical form-building, involving a positive avoidance of gradual transition and a willingness to countenance bold juxtapositions of contrasting elements, that was to find fulfilment in the post-tonal era, in composers as different as Stravinsky and Elliott Carter. By contrast, from the works of the late 1840s onwards an increasing tendency towards greater continuity, if not downright organic integration in the Wagnerian sense, can be traced, a tendency that culminates in *Falstaff* (1893). And far from reflecting an uneasy compromise between two opposing tendencies, to conserve separate forms yet to smooth over the gaps between them, Verdi achieves a triumphant synthesis of old and new. In Julian Budden's striking image, as the tradition embodied in the early operas 'decays into uncertainty, Verdi, half vulture, half phoenix, can still draw nourishment from the carcass, at the same time taking ultramontane features into a style sufficiently confident and flexible to assimilate them'. It was that confidence and flexibility that made the Verdian synthesis so successful, and so rich, the occasional hints of rapprochement with Meyerbeer, Gounod, Bizet, Massenet, or even Wagner himself throwing Verdi's own decisive contribution into clearer perspective. Verdi comes nearest to Wagner, and to the idea of musico-poetic synthesis, in his commitment to the 'parola scenica', the closest possible association of text and music in opera. This may in practice focus more on immediate aspects of the relation between individual words or phrases and the musical structures to which they contribute than the musico-poetic synthesis, with its long-term unifying ambitions; but even for Verdi the technical essence of Romanticism was increasing intensity, and that meant increasing organicism – as *Otello* and *Falstaff* magnificently demonstrate.

Verdi received Boito's libretto for *Otello* in 1880, but it was only after the revisions of *Simon Boccanegra* (1881), in which Boito was also involved, and of *Don Carlos* (1882–4) that concentrated work on the new opera began: the music was composed between March 1884 and December 1886, and the first performance took place at La Scala in February 1887. There is little doubt that Boito's Othello is to no small extent – and of necessity, if Verdi was to provide appropriate music – a nineteenth-century adaptation of Shakespeare's character rather than a close equivalent of the original. The result is certainly not a complete divorce from the characteristics of Romantic melodrama, or Romantic pathos, and the relationship between Otello and Desdemona, in particular, has often been criticized for retaining too little of the complexity evident in Shakespeare. Some critics have even argued for a distinction between Boito's relatively plain characterization – for example, in the basic opposition of a vicious, conniving Iago and a confused, vulnerable Otello – and Verdi's musical transformation of this into something more complex, ambiguous and – therefore – more truly Shakespearean.

It is, one might think, not unusual for opera libretti to be less subtle in themselves than is the dramatic result when the text is set to music. But it is difficult to deny that the power as well as the subtlety of *Otello* is most memorably demonstrated in the music for the two main male characters, whose relationship centres round that essential Verdian theme, jealousy. Iago's 'Credo' is perhaps the opera's most forceful demonstration of the composer's personal mastery, presenting an intense moment of experience with all the energetic economy that was always Verdi's hallmark. To compare the 'Credo' with Wagner's monologue – the so-called 'Watch' – for his blackest villain, Hagen, in *Götterdämmerung*, is to see both composers in their element. Hagen broods, and the music, extremely slow and searchingly chromatic, has as inexorable a feeling of forward movement as it has the sense of emerging seamlessly from, and being absorbed back into, the larger design. Iago's music is nothing if not sharp-edged: it lives for the moment, but with total conviction, attacking directly, without calculation, and fitting perfectly into its appointed place. If Hagen casts an implacable spell, Iago throws devastating punches. Iago needs strong cadences to drive home his obsession: Hagen disdains such forthrightness.

It hardly compromises the great originality and supreme independence of Wagner in *Götterdämmerung* and Verdi in *Otello* to make such comparisons, and just as there is more to the final stages of the *Ring* than black hatred, so there is much more to *Otello* than the rhetoric of envy. The love music, and the lyric episodes, have their own clarity and directness, culminating in Desdemona's Willow Song and Prayer, and an ending which, like that of *Aida*, totally shuns those final, hectic orchestral cadences of the earlier tragedies. Here, at last, the element of understatement normally so foreign to Italian opera finds transfiguring expression.

Comparison between *Götterdämmerung* and *Otello* is one thing. Comparison between *Parsifal* and *Falstaff* (despite the common syllable) might seem a good deal less useful, though the fact that both, like many operas, move from tension to reconciliation is evident enough. One aspect of such a comparison will be considered below. Meanwhile, a particularly important conjunction concerns Verdi alone – the way in which, despite the total contrast between the worlds of *Otello* and *Falstaff*, the obsessional jealousy which Iago expresses so trenchantly in the former surfaces with surprising force in the latter, in Ford's Act II monologue. So remarkable is Verdi's response to the Ford–Falstaff relation that one commentator, Graham Bradshaw (see Hepokoski), has argued that Verdi's music in the opera as a whole actually out-Shakespeares Shakespeare (again, with a little help from Boito). Moreover, in doing so the music can be seen – for the first and last time in Verdi's output – as more a 'Realist' mockery of Romanticism than Romantic in itself. The delicate question of the relation of Realism to Romanticism, touched on in Chapter One, will be raised again in Chapter Nine. But as far as *Falstaff* is concerned, and despite the undeniable shift of emphasis, the work surely represents fulfilment rather than contradiction. *Falstaff* is a comedy which by no means rejects either the spirit or the techniques of Verdian Romanticism. Ford, at the height of his folly – and irrespective of whether Verdi intended a note of parody or not – becomes a powerfully moving figure, and the music for the young lovers has a heartfelt delicacy and a touching spontaneity that surely represent the composer's belief that, far from being dead, Romanticism only needed to recall its musical roots (albeit non-Italian ones) to live again.

As suggested earlier, it is *Falstaff* that embodies the formal aspects of the Verdian synthesis most richly. Organic integration is not so rampant as to represent a rejection of tradition: individual numbers and set pieces may no longer be literally separated from one another by emphatic cadences and pauses, but their presence, and the overall employment of a form built up by contrast and juxtaposition rather than by throughcomposed, symphonic processes, are unmistakable. Accusations of Wagnerism in *Otello* and *Falstaff* have long been exposed as ludicrous, not least because such accusations were often made by critics who had clearly invented the wish as well as the deed. Hanslick, however unfair he was to Wagner, never made that mistake with Verdi: he wrote that 'nowhere in *Falstaff* is the voice suffocated or swamped by the orchestra, nowhere is the memory spoonfed by leitmotifs, nowhere is emotion cooled by sophisticated reflexion. And yet the music of *Falstaff* possesses more the character of animated conversation than that of distinctive melody weaving its own beauty.'

For Hanslick, clearly, the *parlante* had got out of hand, and it was not merely Wagnerian progressiveness which he deplored. Verdi himself, near the end of his life, seemed to have no doubts that the problem of modern music lay elsewhere than in any apparent absence of 'distinctive melody'. 'The most serious fault of modern music is the tendency to over-elaborate. Certainly one should explore new avenues, but not at the cost of substituting artificiality and mannerism for the spontaneity of true inspiration. In art . . . simplicity is everything.' To conclude that 'simplicity is everything' may be seriously to oversimplify. And yet Verdi's capacity for a simplicity which never sinks into triviality is perhaps his most personal and (in the best sense) most precious contribution to music as it begins to tire of the more extravagant and extreme forms of Romanticism. Desdemona's Willow Song, and Nannetta's solo (with chorus) in Act III of *Falstaff*, are triumphs of the capacity of pure melody to distil an atmosphere of rapt concentration and refined emotion. In economy and precision they more than match those fierce outbursts of Iago and Ford discussed earlier, and underline the sense of effortless control of means and ends which bespeaks the creative genius in any age. There is nothing comparable in Wagner: he can certainly provide music of heartrending 'innocence' (though usually with an ironic, seductive edge), as for the Rhinemaidens in *Götterdämmerung* or the Flowermaidens in *Parsifal*. But these 'states' are necessarily and brilliantly protracted in a manner Verdi never needed to contemplate. Wagner was no less a master of control – that is, of proportion. But Verdi was able to hold conservative and progressive tendencies in more equal balance (and ultimately synthesize them) than did that other genius, who transformed German Romantic opera into music drama. The essence of Verdi's lyric style informs the situations of his final comedy as profoundly as the essence of Wagner's symphonic techniques permeates the epic events of *Parsifal*. In these two supreme musical works for the stage – with their very different types of happy ending – the Romantic era is at its richest and most resonant.

CHAPTER NINE

From Glinka to Grieg:
crosscurrents in Romantic nationalism

Historians seeking an arresting encapsulation of the entire essential development of Romantic music can do worse than compare Beethoven's *Pathétique* Piano Sonata op. 13 (probably completed in 1798) with Tchaikovsky's *Pathétique* Symphony (1893). There are clear family resemblances in both between thematic ideas expressive of lamentation or foreboding, which can of course be traced in many other works as well. Yet there are also strong contrasts – for example, between the relatively contained expressiveness of the young Beethoven and the altogether looser, breast-beating histrionics of the aging Tchaikovsky. Before 1800 Beethoven was already a master of the pre-eminently Classical art of making all the elements of his structures function as factors contributing significantly to a unity, an overall coherence in which the overriding concern to define and achieve a goal is not made an excuse for trivializing the successive stages of the progress to that goal. Tchaikovsky, by contrast, could well have been, at best, a reluctant symphonist, using the form because the nineteenth century, however anti-Classical in its Romanticism, Realism or Nationalism, had failed to convince itself that the symphony was not the genre in which a composer could give the clearest indication of seriousness and mastery, freed from the demands of plots and texts. Certainly, one cannot imagine Beethoven, however self-critical, bemoaning the fact that 'my *seams* always showed, and there was no organic union between the separate episodes'.

Not surprisingly, historians have differed over whether to take the composer's own valuation seriously or not. Yet few indeed would attempt to claim that Tchaikovsky was a symphonist whose qualities were the same as those of the Classical masters, and it is therefore often implied that his characteristically Russian interest in melody and colour (rather than harmony and form) is the essence, not just of his Russianism, but also of his Romanticism – as is, of course, his tendency to compose episodic rather than integrated symphonic movements.

Even if, as Hans Keller has argued, there is a powerful reshaping of the traditional tonal and thematic relations (and contrasts) in the first movement of the Fourth Symphony, this reinforces the prevailing view of Tchaikovsky as a great Romantic rather than a would-be Classic. More precisely, it identifies the productive tensions between the 'orthodoxies' the composer learned about in his Western-oriented education and the less conventional imperatives of his own instinct and temperament. The great music these tensions helped to produce is perhaps the more impressive in view of that other tension – between homosexuality and social convention, instinct and orthodoxy – which not only plagued the composer throughout his life but also, it now seems certain, led him to end it by suicide. It is not, then, a simple matter of saying that Tchaikovsky thought more about melody and colour than about harmony and form, but that these elements were constantly at war with each other: their relationship had to be established afresh in each composition if that composition was to carry a full emotional charge.

Such tensions, but especially that between Western European and more local characteristics, had been present in Russian music since the time of Mikhail Glinka (1804–57). Though generally acknowledged as the originator of Russian musical nationalism, Glinka spent long periods in Italy, Germany and France, and his 'nationalism' was as much a matter of his individual approach to non-Russian music as of his use of Russian folk idioms. In his first opera, *A Life for the Tsar* (1834–6), despite the evident Russian quality of the melodic writing,

33 The 'good, amiable, . . . rather commonplace' Glinka in Repin's commemorative portrait (1887).

there is a distinctive, Western-style radicalism. Leitmotifs are used as consistently as in any composer (including Spohr) before Wagner: yet this progressiveness is balanced by a thinness of harmony which is undoubtedly Italian in origin. Russian subject-matter does not therefore lead to a total divorce from Western characteristics. Nor does it in *Ruslan and Ludmilla* (1842), a work of great historical influence and significance that is also a failure, as drama. Its impact outside Russia lies in harmonic progressions bold enough to have influenced Liszt. But Glinka's was not a temperament likely to result in music of consistent originality, and it seems clear that the very incompleteness of his achievement, and his reflection of musical personalities stronger than his own, provided a greater stimulus to those who came after him than mastery and individuality could possibly have done. Berlioz recognized Glinka's chameleon-like personality when he wrote (diplomatically?) in 1845 that 'his talent is essentially supple and varied; his style has the rare distinction of changing itself at the composer's will according to the requirements and character of the subject he is treating'. Tchaikovsky, an enthusiast, described the Glinka paradox well in a letter: 'When you read his *Memoirs*, which reveal a good, amiable, but empty and rather commonplace man: when you play his slighter compositions, it is just not possible to believe that all these were written by the very same man who created, for example, . . . the "Slavsya" Chorus!' (in *A Life for the Tsar*) or that 'stunningly original piece' *Karaminskaya*.

It could of course be argued that Glinka's failure fully to integrate Russian-style melodic material with the developing conventions of German and Italian opera was the kind of necessary 'failure' that persists throughout the history of Russian art music. Certainly, attempts to give Russian opera a more profoundly national character by stressing the natural rhythms of the text were not to achieve any lasting success either. But Glinka's stature as an innovator and originator is the more noteworthy since he emerged from a country with no tradition of serious musical education. Systematic instruction in composition or musical theory only became generally available in 1859, with the founding of the Russian Musical Society in St Petersburg, and the Society also generated that intriguing, infuriating rivalry between a pro-Western faction in Russian musical life (led by the founder of the Russian Musical Society, Anton Rubinstein) and the nationalist factions, headed by Serov and Balakirev.

Yet the core of the dispute was less between pro- and anti-nationalist forces than between those who believed in orthodox musical education and those who did not, as well as between adherents of Mendelssohn on the one hand and Wagner or Liszt on the other. Mily Balakirev (1837–1910) set himself up as the very model of post-1850s radicalism: although such titles as sonata, symphony and concerto are to be found among his works he would argue that the only worthwhile music was programmatic, and his advocacy of 'formlessness' for the music of the future stemmed from a vision of extending the freedoms won by the earlier Romantics he most admired – Berlioz, Liszt and Schumann, as well as their great predecessors, Weber, Schubert and late Beethoven. Balakirev did not include Wagner in his modern pantheon, no doubt because his arch-rival Serov had already established himself as the principal Russian advocate of Wagner in the 1860s; also, perhaps, as a reflection of his own failure to complete an opera. Balakirev as a composer is probably at his finest in his piano music, notably the 'oriental fantasy' *Islamey* (first version, 1869), which stands comparison with Liszt's best virtuoso piano works. Although he was certainly a nationalist, his was a nationalism derived from the innovative potential found in Glinka rather than in the resources of Russian folk music. The emphasis was on the radical rather than the national – although in practice Russian subjects and folk-influenced melodic materials did play a vital part in the music of Balakirev and his associates.

For about eight years after the founding of the Russian Musical Society in 1859 Balakirev's influence – especially on Borodin (1833–87), Cui (1835–1918), Musorgsky (1839–81) and Rimsky-Korsakov (1844–1908), who, with him, made up the famous 'Five' – was immense. In 1869 Tchaikovsky described him as 'narrow-minded' and 'stubborn', and yet 'an honest and good man, and as an artist [he] soars above the ordinary level'. And Rimsky-Korsakov claimed that 'his influence over those around him was boundless, and resembled some magnetic or mesmeric force'. That influence therefore helped to contribute much to the distinctive qualities of Russian Romantic music. Yet the products of Rubinstein's Conservatoire were by no means anti-Romantic either: Tchaikovsky was one of the first batch of graduates. The most notable developments in Russian composition were therefore less a matter of conflicts between pro-Balakirev radicals and pro-Rubinstein

34 The suitably exotic title-page of Balakirev's oriental fantasy *Islamey* – the revised edition of 1902.

conservatives (a relatively short-lived conflict anyway: by 1871 Balakirev's pupil Rimsky-Korsakov was teaching at the St Petersburg Conservatoire) than of the attempts to develop what is usually known as a thoroughgoing 'Realist' musical style.

At its most extreme, as in Dargomïzhsky's *The Stone Guest* (which he worked on throughout the 1860s), Realism involved the kind of naturalism which, at the very least, was likely to act as a check on the free musical fantasy so essential to Romanticism: opera was seen as in no sense superior to spoken drama, and in both, it was felt, the aim should be the expressive rendering of the text. Moreover, the issue was not simply one of faithfulness to textual tone and rhythm. The emotions themselves must be rendered as faithfully – as 'scientifically' – as possible. Such concern with the precise details of verbal and expressive inflections was indeed remote from the grand vistas and broad effects on which Romanticism thrived, at least after 1850; and the logical result of a true musical Realism would have been a thoroughgoing, totally consistent and explicit 'language', a music in which what was being expressed was always unambiguously clear to all. Yet it is perhaps hardly surprising that, even in Russia, this ideal was never attained: admiration of and stimulation by the major Romantic masters was a more crucial factor in the development of the best Russian composers than willingness to shackle their musical instincts in the abject service of texts. Dargomïzhsky himself, in *The Stone Guest*, produced an essentially lyrical melodic line, and it might well be thought that in his search for a greater fidelity to the nuances of the text he was simply matching Wagner's theoretical ideal. The main difference between Dargomïzhsky's Realism and Wagner's word–tone synthesis was that, while the Russian sought to emphasize the vocal lines, he also sought to restrain the contribution of the orchestra. Had this attempt to stem the tide of nineteenth-century musical evolution succeeded it would indeed have stopped Romanticism – or Romantic opera, at any rate – in its tracks. As it is, Russian theorists and composers seem nowhere more absurd, or more out of touch with reality, than when proclaiming that Wagner was in no sense a proper opera composer. The most telling example of Russian Realism is Musorgsky's *Marriage*, a setting of Gogol, which, incomplete though it is, indicates that a serious attempt at Realism could provide a broader stimulus for experiment whose influence might be considerable, reaching fulfilment in the anti-Romantic twentieth century. *The Stone Guest* itself had a more immediate influence, however: the greatest nineteenth-century Russian opera, Musorgsky's *Boris Godunov*, might well not have taken the form it did but for Dargomïzhsky's example, for all that *Boris* and its successor *Khovanshchina* also owe to the conventions of grand opera.

Lacking clearly directed musical education, Musorgsky's early development had been nothing if not cosmopolitan; he was influenced by Meyerbeer, Schumann and Liszt as well as Glinka and Balakirev. Yet after a visit to Moscow at the age of twenty in 1859 he declared: 'I have been a cosmopolitan, but now there's been some sort of regeneration. Everything Russian is becoming dear to me.' It was nine years after that, in 1868, that he abandoned work on *Marriage*: as he said in letters at the time, 'if you dismiss operatic tradition altogether, and can imagine musical dialogue staged as uncomplicated conversation, then *Marriage* is an opera'. But it was also 'a cage in which I have been locked until I am tamed; then I can be free'.

At this stage of his development Musorgsky was acutely conscious of what he saw as the dangers of essentially alien traditions: he accused Rimsky-Korsakov of 'germanizing' – 'he repeats over and over what has been said' – and later asserted that 'the Germans, from their shoe leather fried in lard to Wagner's seven-hour opera, offer nothing that *I* like . . . The most talented Germans – Beethoven, Weber, and Schumann – were (each in his own way) poor vocal composers'. It was in connection with *Marriage* that Musorgsky gave his clearest definition of what musical Realism involved: 'Here is what I would like: for my characters to speak on stage as people speak in real life, and besides this for the appearance and power of the character's intonation, supported by the orchestra's formation of a musical outline of their speech, to achieve their aim directly. That is, my music should be an artistic reproduction of human speech in all of its most subtle nuances. In other words, *the sounds of human speech* as outward manifestations of thought and feeling must, without exaggeration or coercion, become music that is true and accurate – but artistic, highly artistic.'

Such ambitions met with widespread disapproval, and a review of 1870 accused the composer of 'an excessive desire to be original', as well as of 'the crudest realism, approaching cynicism'. Nothing daunted, Musorgsky, in 1875, provided a still broader statement of radical intent: 'The artist cannot run away from the outside world; even in the nuances of subjective creativity there are reflections of impressions of the outside world. Just don't lie – speak the truth . . . Artistic truth cannot tolerate predetermined forms; life is varied and often capricious . . . Rarely does one create a living phenomenon or character in a form unique to it, one no other artist has used before . . . This is the sort of thing I am pregnant with at present.' He returned to the point again in the third-person *Autobiographical Sketch* prepared near the end of his life: 'Proceeding from the conviction that human speech is strictly controlled by musical laws, he considers the task of the art of music to be the reproduction in musical sounds, not only of the mood of feeling, but principally of the mood of human speech.'

Given such preoccupations, it may seem surprising that Musorgsky should have abandoned *Marriage* for a project that, while enabling him to achieve his ambition of breaking decisively with existing conventions, nevertheless depended for its success (in its 'final' form, at least) on a conjunction between Realism and grand-operatic

35 Musorgsky. Fervent nationalist, aspiring Realist, who, in *Boris Godunov*, transformed Romantic opera from within.

Romanticism, rather than an outright rejection of the latter. *Boris Godunov* is remarkable for the way these different features coexist and balance out. It is highly original in its avoidance of simple linear continuity. In his selection from the twenty-four scenes of Pushkin's original text, the composer disdained – at least in his first version of the opera – to establish the kind of dramatic unity and process that might seem like 'germanizing'. And even in the form in which the work was eventually performed it struck one of Musorgsky's most implacable opponents, the critic Herman Laroche, as a work in which 'the scenes are barely stitched together at all'. Nevertheless, *Boris* was a great deal more than a Realist pageant, or national chronicle. It has characters with remarkably varied and sharply drawn identities, and its treatment of Boris's own personal tragedy gives the Tsar a stature in which comparisons with Verdi's Otello or Wagner's Wotan are not inappropriate. By transcending so many of its models and sources, and standing aside from some of the most fundamental notions of musical structuring prevalent at the time, the opera naturally transforms the idea of Romanticism itself: but it does so from within. The personal tragedy of Boris, and the collective suffering of the Russian people, are not the stuff of anti-Romanticism.

Musorgsky's greatness lay in his supreme embodiment of Balakirev's 'modernist' principle: he was no absolute musician. Yet such an exclusive commitment to the programmatic was rare, even in Russia, and most composers of this period felt obliged to attempt some rapprochement with 'abstraction' in the form of non-programmatic instrumental forms. Rarely did the resulting music have an emotional quality suggesting total surrender to the spirit of Romanticism. Apart from certain works by Tchaikovsky, perhaps the most intensely Romantic Russian music is by Borodin – not least in the way the Second Symphony (completed in 1876) displays the organic integration and emotional intensity of the best Western examples of the period. Yet for all its reflection of the general, radical High Romantic fascination with texts and programmes, Russian music can display a quality which seems strongly to anticipate twentieth-century anti-Romanticism, as incarnated by Stravinsky. It is no doubt appropriate that, of all the late-Romantic Russians, it is Stravinsky's teacher Rimsky-Korsakov who, in *Sheherazade*, *Snowmaiden*, *The Golden Cockerel*, and other major works should anticipate most clearly that glassy glitter, that sense of the fantastic caught in a set of dazzling mechanisms in which genuine emotion is frozen – not excluded, but laid out for inspection – which Stravinsky made the basis for his great anti-Romantic initiative. Yet Stravinsky himself was a passionate admirer of Tchaikovsky, and Tchaikovsky was undoubtedly the greatest Russian composer before Stravinsky precisely because his music had so wide a range of technical and expressive reference. Not simply Russian, it was also far from straightforwardly 'European'. And if it was, pre-eminently, Romantic, it did not exclude contacts with the kind of vanished clarity and equilibrium that Tchaikovsky himself associated primarily with Mozart.

Pyotr Ilyich Tchaikovsky (1840–93) was often at odds with his Russian contemporaries. The critic Laroche, noting the absence of vulgarity in his music, deemed him 'a civilized man', which fits well alongside Tchaikovsky's own claim, in 1874, that he consigned *Boris Godunov* 'to the devil; it is the most vulgar and foul parody of music'. Civilization also meant taking the symphony seriously, and from the very beginning of his career when, at the prompting of Nikolay Rubinstein, he embarked on his first attempt at the form, there can be no mistaking Tchaikovsky's acceptance of the – in essence, German –

argument that this was the form in which the composer should be able to express the fullest mastery and originality. Later critics – not overlooking parallels with Tchaikovsky's apparently reluctant homosexuality – have occasionally seen this struggle with the symphony as a lifelong battle to come to terms with something frightening yet inescapable: after all, the composer did acknowledge in a letter of 1872 that 'I do not exactly find my work as a composer particularly soothing'. Occasionally the battle was well and truly lost: the first movement of the First Symphony, for example, not only lacks that purposeful organicism which Classical models provide, but quite fails to compensate for its episodic harmonic character by the kind of thematic interrelationships that a more successful sonata structure like the first movement of the Second String Quartet (completed 1874) achieves. Nor were Tchaikovsky's difficulties in achieving appropriate formal integration confined to 'abstract' compositions. In the Fantasy-Overture *Romeo and Juliet* (first version 1869–70) he produced his first masterpiece, whose programmaticism is perhaps the more poignant because the tragic heterosexual love it depicts was utterly remote from his own experience. But the greatness of *Romeo and Juliet* has much to do with the presence of precisely that sense of purposeful progression that the composer found so hard to recapture in his later tone-poems, including the notably inorganic symphonic fantasia *Francesca da Rimini* (1876).

As suggested earlier, in the discussion of Verdi, too much can be made of the apparent traumas Romantic composers experienced in their quest for the organic, when their instincts were encouraging them to exploit the effective and satisfying tension between, for example, a 'mosaic' approach to form and tonal planning and an integrated or cyclic thematic process. Of course, Tchaikovsky may genuinely have believed that his 'seams showed' more reprehensibly than those of, say, Berlioz or Liszt. If so, his tenacity was the more remarkable, for he allowed himself only intermittent escape from contemporary 'problems' into works like *Mozartiana* and the *Rococo Variations*. It was his determination in facing the issue of the present, of writing symphonic and theatrical works acknowledging the Russian folk and art heritage but not seeking to evade the stronger traditions of non-Russian art music that makes his overall achievement such a heroic one. With the First Piano Concerto, the last three numbered symphonies, and the *Manfred* Symphony, he

138

proved that he was unequalled in Russia in his ability to reinterpret and explore the traditions of symphonic design and expression.

The operas are uneven: after 1876, when he heard both the *Ring* and *Carmen*, he had no doubt that his sympathies lay entirely with Bizet, claiming that 'Bizet is an artist who in spite of paying tribute to the decadent taste of this century is full of sincere feeling and inspiration.' But it was precisely the 'colder' aspects of *Carmen* – the detachment which makes its impact all the greater – that Tchaikovsky found difficult to match in his own operas. At his best, as in the letter scene in *Eugene Onegin* (1879), there is a powerful yet freshly minted lyric impulse that is utterly personal. *The Queen of Spades* (1890) is more ambitious – and less consistent in quality, though equally impressive at its best, and with strikingly original passages, not least the austerely solemn ending. Even so, it was as a ballet composer that Tchaikovsky excelled; here he could exploit his skill for the evocation of atmosphere in purely orchestral terms, with that degree of rhythmic and structural formality that accompaniment to dance requires. There are enough purely musical virtues – unfailingly well-characterized ideas, flexible yet well-balanced forms – to make *The Sleeping Beauty* (1889) the finest of all Tchaikovsky's works for the

Ballet

36 A scene from the original production (1890) at the Maryinsky Theatre, St Petersburg, of Tchaikovsky's ballet *The Sleeping Beauty*.

stage, superior to both the earlier *Swan Lake* (1876) and the later *Nutcracker* (1892) and, ultimately, to all the operas: indeed, it has been argued that Tchaikovsky never surpassed *The Sleeping Beauty* in any other genre.

Alongside the *Pathétique* Symphony, of course, *The Sleeping Beauty* may seem the ultimate in escapist entertainment. As he worked rapidly on the *Pathétique* (1893), the composer wrote that 'I am very proud of my new symphony, and think it is my best work.' And while, like many composers, he usually felt the current work in progress to be 'the best', Tchaikovsky was sufficiently shrewd and sensitive to know when he was creating something strong enough to be considered in its own terms and not merely in relation to traditions and models whose relevance was insufficiently questioned. As this symphony shows, Tchaikovsky could express aspects of the 'Romantic agony' as powerfully and memorably as Wagner in *Tristan* or Verdi in *Otello*. And he could do so through an interpretation of symphonic processes which is invalid only if inflexible and unimaginative notions of inviolable Classical procedures and proportions are invoked. The presence of very

37 Photograph of Tchaikovsky, *c.* 1890, his fiftieth year, which saw the première of *The Sleeping Beauty* and the composition and première of his ninth opera, *The Queen of Spades*.

definite 'seams' – especially between the main sections of the outer movements – actually contributes to that sense of conflict and dramatic confrontation: of coherence challenged but ultimately maintained, of the search for lyric poise constantly threatened by emotional catastrophe, which is the essence of Tchaikovsky's greatness.

Although, by comparison with Moscow and St Petersburg, Prague is on the doorstep of Vienna, Weimar and Bayreuth, the two greatest Czech Romantics – Bedřich Smetana (1824–84) and Antonín Dvořák (1841–1904) – seem to have found it easier than their Russian contemporaries to pursue nationalist ideals without at the same time needing to reject the powerful influences emanating from close by. The growth of national feeling in what remained provinces of the Habsburg Empire until 1918 did not promote any attempt to reject or obliterate the strong cultural traditions which had made Prague such a significant musical centre in the later eighteenth century. If anything, the establishment of a conservatoire there in 1811 (although composition as such was not taught until much later), as well as a

38 Czech nationalism. A contemporary engraving of a barricade in the Old Town, Prague, during the 1848 disturbances. Czechoslovakia remained part of the Hapsburg Empire until 1918.

permanent opera company and various concert-giving organizations, reinforced the non-Czech factor in the city's musical life: and it was not until Smetana began to write stage works in the 1860s that a composer emerged who was capable of satisfying the desire of the local nationalities for an operatic idiom that was truly Czech.

Smetana's own musical language had strong roots outside his native land. At the age of sixteen he heard, and was enslaved by, Liszt's playing, and the two became firm friends. Smetana attended the first performance of the *Faust* Symphony in Weimar, and it was under the influence of the Lisztian style of programme music that his own career as a composer of symphonic poems was launched – with *Richard III* (1858). (Earlier, his music reflected an admiration for Schumann: Smetana had met Robert and Clara in Prague in 1847, and the Piano Trio of 1855 is probably the work of Smetana's in which Schumann's influence is most productively present.) The loose form and reliance on repetition rather than transformation in *Richard III* are indeed characteristic of Liszt – at his worst. But in *Hakon Jarl* (1861–2) Smetana achieved a more convincingly integrated form. It is in any case ironic, given Smetana's great gifts, that his reputation as a disciple of Liszt should have hindered his career in Czechoslovakia. Around 1860 he was felt to be insufficiently nationalist, whatever the purely musical worth of his work. And accusations of excessive foreign influence were to bedevil his later career as an opera composer – ironically, again, since his avowed aim was to do as much as he could to promote the musical expression of national feeling.

In a review of July 1864 Smetana left a vivid account of the difficulties of performing opera at Prague's Provisional Theatre. 'How can we possibly play opera in a house as small as ours? In *Les Huguenots*, the armies barely number eight on each side . . . and thus provoke laughter. The singers are pressed so close together in the foreground that everyone must be careful not to hurt his neighbour when he turns.' Smetana nevertheless decided to tackle the medium, and his own early operas were *The Brandenburgers in Bohemia* (completed in 1863, when it won a competition for an opera on a Czech theme, and first performed in 1866) and *The Bartered Bride* (first version completed and performed in 1866). Both were successful – the latter not at first – but difficulties arose when Smetana sought to deal with more ambitious nationalist projects. *Dalibor* (first performed in 1868) and *Libuše* (completed in 1872, not performed

39 Title-page of the two-piano arrangement of Smetana's *Vltava*. Such arrangements of orchestral scores were a valuable way of increasing their accessibility.

until 1881) tackled heroic, epic themes, and the first brought the inevitable accusations of Wagnerism. One can see why, and yet to categorize these works as Wagnerian is to use that term very loosely. The 'Wagnerian' technique of recurring themes stems rather from Liszt: and while *Libuše*, which Smetana defiantly claimed in 1882 as 'the highest peak in the expression of Czech music' may at times recall *Die Meistersinger*, it also confirms that Smetana, quite unlike Wagner, is at his best when chromaticism is kept firmly under control, enhancing the freshness of his essentially diatonic melodic invention (and consonant harmony). Smetana's later operas *The Kiss* (1875–6) and *The Devil's Wall* (1879–82) also display the 'Wagnerian' virtues of a strong sense of continuity, often vested in skilfully contrived transitions.

But it is the dance-like, diatonic music in the operas which shows the composer at his most personal, and the presence of these qualities on the smaller scale of the later tone poems provides the real fulfilment of epic, Romantic breadth and personal nationalist allusion in Smetana. The reputation of the cycle of six tone poems, *Má vlast* (1872–9), has probably suffered in the twentieth century from the extreme popularity of one item – *Vltava*. As a whole, however, the cycle is remarkably ambitious and powerful. The six pieces are scarcely unified in the sense of forming some kind of extended symphony, but the relative looseness of overall design is, in fact, an advantage, and there are, in any case, a number of motivic cross-references. *Má vlast* is superior to the great majority of Liszt's tone poems and symphonic works (which, of course, preceded it) not least because there is little attempt to provide post-Beethovenian motivic processes appropriate to the 1870s. In sharp contrast to Liszt, Smetana tends to use broad, well-shaped melodies, full of 'national' spirit (the 'Vltava' theme itself has been shown to derive from a *Swedish* folksong) and even an actual hymn tune. The noble, eminently Romantic atmosphere which can result is evident at once in the first movement, *Vyšehrad*, whose bardic, poetic tone is far removed from the world of the symphony. The passionate *Šarka* is in many ways the most overtly dramatic and forceful of the six, generating great energy, while *From Bohemia's Woods and Fields* has the most haunting melodic material. The last, linked pair of movements, *Tábor* and *Blaník*, are often said to mark a falling-off, yet they are fascinating and compelling, almost like Romantic chorale fantasias in their use of a Hussite hymn whose melody absorbs smaller motifs into itself. Whatever Smetana's debts to Liszt, or Berlioz, he seems – notably in *Blaník* – to foreshadow the style (not the form) of Bruckner, who composed the first versions of his third, fourth and fifth symphonies during the period 1873–6.

An indication of the contemporary impact – and the effect of the nationalism – of this music outside Czechoslovakia can be found in Hugo Wolf's account of the Viennese première of *Vyšehrad* and *Vltava* in November 1886: 'Since the composer uses Slavic airs in both works, we cannot speak of his powers of invention. But the treatment of the themes discloses so much intelligence and musico-poetic sensibility that we were sheerly astonished to be meeting so gifted a composer in the concert hall for the first time. His command of form, moreover, is amazing, and his instrumentation of the order of Berlioz. In short, we have here two masterpieces.' Wolf surely exaggerates the 'Slavic' nature of Smetana's material in these works. He did use genuine folk materials in his later operas *The Kiss* and *The Two Widows* (1873–4), and in some of his Czech Dances (1878–9). In general, however, the nationalism of his music depends more on his own personal response to such folk materials than on their direct

40 Pencil drawing of Dvořák in later life: a relatively rare hint of a more serious frame of mind.

quotation. Smetana's achievement in this respect must have acted as an inspiring example to the young Dvořák, whose own style developed as a completely personal response to a wide range of national and international features. The main difference between Smetana and Dvořák is that, while the younger man also failed to match the success of Verdi and Wagner in the theatre, he made a much more considerable contribution to the medium of symphonic music, even when the greatness of *Má vlast* is acknowledged. Dvořák also achieved extraordinary success abroad.

In a letter written from New York in 1893 Dvořák commented: 'If in my own career I have achieved a measure of success and reward it is to some extent due to the fact that I was the son of poor parents and was reared in an atmosphere of struggle and endeavour.' Dvořák emphasized the strains to which his lack of education and resources had exposed him: 'I can hardly understand how I endured the privations and labour of my youth. Could I have had . . . the advantages, freely offered in such a school as the National Conservatory of Music, I might have been spared many of my hardest trials, and have accomplished much more. Not that I was unable to produce music, but that I had not technique enough to express all that was in me. I had ideas but I could not utter them perfectly.'

145

'Struggle' is indeed a vital component of Romanticism. Yet it may be surprising to find Dvořák giving such emphasis to it. Perhaps he could already sense that posterity would jump to conclusions about his apparently easy fertility and geniality. For all his unpropitious background, and his experience in marriage of that most tragic aspect of pre-twentieth-century family life – a high degree of infant mortality – Dvořák seems the very model of the stable and successful bourgeois man of music, able to make a living from the fruits of his labours without being chained to the service of any individual or institution. He was undoubtedly fortunate to find generous patronage, especially in America: and although his professional life had its share of conflicts – not with princes but with a publisher (Simrock) – he was in the ideal position of being able to supply what the 'market' required in all genres, from Slavonic Dances to symphonies and operas, in an idiom that was acceptably accessible and satisfyingly personal. While in no sense an experimenter – he did not seek to create new forms or challenge existing norms of dissonance or periodicity – he was able to move effectively and individually within existing conventions. His distinction lies in the fact that his fluent, fresh, flexible idiom so rarely becomes routine. There is an air of spontaneity and a palpable creative energy in Dvořák's music that raise him well above the status of a minor master. He was undoubtedly fortunate in being able to profit from the battles fought by others – Smetana, in particular. But he was never content with the complaisant role of the camp-follower. His creative vitality and expressive vision were both substantial and sustained enough to ensure that he became a true Romantic, even if of a relatively conservative cast.

Wagner was in many ways Dvořák's attendant musical deity, and became so when the young Czech encountered the music as a sixteen-year-old violist in Prague's St Cecilia Society Orchestra. Although that enthusiasm had an unfortunate effect on several early compositions, for example, the opera *Alfred* (1870), and was submerged in the more Classically orientated scores of his maturity, it re-emerged more productively at the end of his life in the operas *Rusalka* (1900) and *Armida* (1902–3). Dvořák's work is a good illustration of the extent to which it was possible to be influenced by Wagnerian methods – declamatory vocal writing and the 'symphonic' treatment of leitmotifs – without becoming a slave to

Wagner's actual harmonic style. Moreover, by the time Dvořák was able to exploit Wagnerian methods convincingly – as, for example, in *Rusalka* – the result (appropriately, for its date) seems if anything closer in style to Richard Strauss than to the Magician of Bayreuth. However potent the Wagner connection, therefore, it was for long periods unobtrusive, and is scarcely detectable at all in Dvořák's very finest works, like the Symphony no. 7 or the Cello Concerto. It is the compositions in symphonic forms – symphonies, concertos and various chamber compositions – which ensure Dvořák a place with the great masters. And his predilection for the symphony was pre-eminently the result of his admiration for Mozart, Beethoven and Schubert – reinforced, later, by his friendship, and artistic kinship, with Brahms.

Symphonic mastery was not achieved without effort, and the Fifth Symphony of 1875 is the first in which Dvořák's own personal voice is unmistakably present. Three years later, there came a spate of works which reveal an equally personal nationalism. Though Dvořák rarely borrowed directly from folk music, there are unmistakable national features, not just of melody but also of rhythm, as in the furiant and dumka movements in the Serenade for Wind, the Sextet op. 48 and the E flat String Quartet, as well as in the various Slavonic Dances and rhapsodies. In Dvořák's greatest works, however, such features are fully absorbed into a language suitable for symphonic processes, and even in a composition as full of Czech feeling as the Symphony no. 8 the lyrical and dance-like qualities serve a distinctive and substantial symphonic argument. Nor is it the least of Dvořák's achievements that he could – in what many would claim to be his finest single work, the Symphony no. 7 (1885) – reflect the influence of Brahms in a perfectly natural way, so that it becomes an extension – a deepening – of his own personal idiom.

In character Dvořák could scarcely have been more different from Brahms: for example, he was deeply religious and distressed by Brahms's agnosticism. Dvořák was also deeply patriotic, yet spent long periods abroad, and enjoyed great success in England and America, as well as nearer home in Austria and Germany. He may indeed have been a more conventional man than most of his fellow Romantics, and have lived a less turbulent life. He did nevertheless suffer anxieties – not just the kind of concern about his family's health which was all too understandable at the time, but less rational fears:

there are signs of agoraphobia, and he disliked making long journeys alone. Even so, it is scarcely possible to cast him in the role of rival to Tchaikovsky as Romantic neurotic, and it is more important not to assume that the much prized geniality and spontaneity of his music were the result of totally effortless inspiration. Some of his finest works, such as the Cello Concerto (1896), were the product of much sketching and revision, even if the end-result bears few signs of the stresses and strains of creative decision-making or agonizing over alternatives. Dvořák was able to build unobtrusive yet effective formal frameworks and devise the most suitable harmonic contexts for the unfolding and interaction of thematic ideas, so that the lyric impulse was neither thwarted nor allowed to vitiate the necessary progress of organic symphonic design. Yet, as a true Romantic, Dvořák was not interested in harmony or tonality for its own sake: indeed, his harmony was in general less progressive than Smetana's, reflecting the Schubertian rather than Lisztian (or Wagnerian) sources of his language.

For historians inclined to see the essence of Romanticism in non-symphonic music (save for the tone poems or the freer sonata structures of Liszt), and the whole nineteenth-century symphonic tradition as a decline from the standards set by Beethoven, even Dvořák may, like Tchaikovsky, stand accused of 'loose structure'. Yet if it is of the essence that nineteenth-century music sought to reduce the structural significance of harmony and tonality – to escape the confines of Classical discipline – it is inevitable that, judged by Classical standards, it will seem more concerned with parts than with wholes. We can only condemn it for allowing the 'seams' to show if we can be sure that a Romantic style with a fully integrated structure after the Classical ideal was actually possible, or necessary.

Although it now seems as if Czech music after Smetana and Dvořák was dominated by Janáček (who was born only thirteen years after Dvořák, in 1854), Janáček did not achieve full prominence until after 1918. Two other composers made a particular contribution to the continuation of Czech Romanticism: Vitězslav Novák (1870–1949), primarily through his symphonic poems, and Josef Suk (1874–1935), Dvořák's son-in-law and widely seen as his successor. Like Janáček, Suk developed gradually from a Romantic style – that of the Serenade for Strings (1892) – to something much more radical. On a larger scale, Suk's *Asrael* Symphony (1905–6) has had great claims made on its behalf, and it certainly justifies the comparisons with Mahler's expressive power and formal clarity. Suk was no nationalist: his compositions do not reflect the influence of folk music, and in his relative lack of explicit 'Czechness' he recalls an earlier, no less significant figure, Zdeněk Fibich (1850–1900). Fibich studied in western Europe, including a spell in Leipzig with Moscheles when the inevitable influence of Mendelssohn made itself felt: and although he wrote a 'nationalist' tone poem in 1873, before Smetana completed *Má vlast*, he seemed in general less of a nationalist than his two greater contemporaries. By comparison with Smetana and Dvořák, Fibich, for all his undoubted Romanticism, was less individual as well as less evidently Czech. So, despite the fact that *The Bride of Messina* (1882–3) has been proposed as the best Czech opera of the century, and despite his activity in the field of melodrama, Fibich – whether through 'cosmopolitanism' or sheer lack of musical character – has been largely neglected since his death.

Scandinavia may have produced no musicians in the nineteenth century to equal such literary giants as Ibsen or Strindberg, yet one composer – Grieg – is arguably more important than commonly acknowledged: and there are others deserving more attention than they currently receive. In Sweden Franz Berwald (1796–1868) is certainly not negligible, and his four symphonies (1842–5) make a distinctive contribution to the genre as it evolves from Mendelssohn and Schumann towards Dvořák and Brahms. It is significant that Berwald's music was rather more successful in Vienna than it was in Sweden; the problem of being a prophet without honour in his own country was a common one. Niels Gade (1817–90) was of great importance to music in Denmark, yet he achieved his main successes in Leipzig, where Mendelssohn performed his first symphony in 1843, and in 1847 he became Mendelssohn's successor as chief conductor of the Gewandhaus orchestra. Gade returned to Denmark in 1848, but his musical language remained more Romantic than nationalist, and he himself became sceptical of the kind of National Romanticism, based in Norway and evident in Grieg and Svendsen, whose music increasingly tended to overshadow his own.

Like Fibich and Gade and many others, Edvard Grieg (1843–1907) had studied in Leipzig; but it seems clear that a local Norwegian

The text on the programme reads:

L'ŒUVRE : 22, Rue Turgot

PEER GYNT

Poème dramatique en 5 actes

d'Henrik-Ibsen, Musique de E. Grieg
Traduction de M. le Comte PROZOR
Orchestre conduit par M. Gabriel Marie
Sous la Voûte par M. Hoffbach

41 Programme by Edvard Munch for performances of Ibsen's *Peer Gynt*, with Grieg's music, Paris 1896.

composer like J. P. E. Hartmann was a more constructive influence on him than, for example, Gade, who, when Grieg moved to Copenhagen in 1863, advised him to attempt a symphony: in making the attempt, Grieg learned the hard way that such substantial structures were not for him, and the relatively early Piano Concerto of 1868 remained his best attempt at a traditional large-scale design; he was never to achieve anything comparable in later life.

Grieg's devotion to his native land was intense, and he was much stimulated in his earlier years by contact with traditional music, and with important local musicians like Ole Bull and Richard Nordraak. The frustrations of life in a country with few traditions and poor facilities were nevertheless considerable, and hardly helped to encourage Grieg's creativity. As a result he was a frequent traveller to such centres as Leipzig, Paris and Vienna, and he found much satisfaction in encounters with such contemporary masters as Brahms and Tchaikovsky, as well as in hearing his own works better performed than was usually the case in Norway.

The sheer range of Grieg's musical enthusiasms might seem a recipe for lack of creative purposefulness: he found things to praise in Schumann and Franck, Wagner and Verdi, Bizet and Brahms. And yet, as a miniaturist, especially in the field of song, his achievement was considerable. It is often the more progressive aspects of his musical language which receive most critical attention – the pre-Debussy 'impressionism', the pre-Bartók diatonic dissonances – and these are certainly striking and impressive. Yet his essential Romanticism stems from the fact that such progressiveness was the exception, not the rule. He did not become so radical a folklorist that his harmony became entirely 'empirical'; and in any case, particularly in such late works as the Norwegian Folk Tunes (1896) and the *Slåtter* for Piano (1902), it was more a matter of close affinity with traditional Norwegian music than direct quotation or adaptation of it.

Hackneyed though it can often seem today, Grieg's incidental music for *Peer Gynt* (1874–5) is a fine example of the freshness, vitality and lyric eloquence he could bring to orchestral music. Nevertheless, it is in Grieg's songs – for example the twelve settings of Vinje, op. 33, and the superb *Haugtussa* cycle, op. 67 (1895), with its powerful evocation of the trials of disappointed love – that we find his most memorable and personal Romanticism. These songs are still neglected, due more than anything to the difficulty of producing singing texts in any language other than the original. But until they are more widely known our picture of this allegedly familiar composer remains sadly incomplete.

CHAPTER TEN

Along the fringe:
late Romantic music in Britain, France and America

It was only when the great central achievements of Romanticism could be viewed retrospectively that British composers – Edward Elgar (1857–1934) and Frederick Delius (1862–1934), pre-eminently – emerged with the ability to add something personal and memorable to them. The earlier, and major, part of the nineteenth century is commonly characterized as a time of missed opportunities in British music, and of craven subordination to foreign influences (Mendelssohn, Gounod), as well as of sheer incompatibility between the ethics of Victorianism and the aesthetics of Romanticism. During the 1830s it seemed for a while that British composers would make as notable a contribution to the development of Romanticism in music as British poets had to literary Romanticism. Sadly, the promise was not fulfilled. Two potentially interesting figures, Robert Lucas Pearsall and Henry Hugo Pierson, left the country but never made substantial reputations abroad: others, like Samuel Sebastian Wesley and William Sterndale Bennett, who remained in England and were relatively successful, might well have achieved even more in a more propitious cultural climate.

A British contribution to the early development of Romanticism can be claimed if John Field is so designated; he was born in Dublin in 1782, but lived in London from 1793 to 1802 before settling in Russia. It is Field's nocturnes (the first composed in 1812) which initiated this most Romantic of genres, and even if the form is chauvinistically claimed as a British (or Irish) invention, its influence in Britain itself was hardly momentous; indeed, it now seems probable that the German-born but British-resident J. B. Cramer had a more palpable effect on the development of native keyboard composition – notably on the work of William Sterndale Bennett. Bennett was one of the few with the ability to absorb the impact of Cramer and Mendelssohn – the first performance of *Elijah* at Birmingham in 1846 was probably the highpoint of continental influence in nineteenth-century Britain – without seeming an abject and inferior imitator. Not only did

Bennett have some success as a composer of 'Romantic concert overtures' like *The Tempest* and *The Wood-Nymphs*, but one 'abstract' work, at least, the Sonata Duo for cello and piano (1852) displays a real ability to compose on a satisfyingly substantial scale.

Such achievements in the realm of orchestral and instrumental music were exceptional – and the prospects for a fully-fledged British Romantic opera were even less propitious. What passes for 'English Romantic opera' deserves the term more for its subject-matter than for its music, which never matched the expressive force and dramatic conviction, with respect both to the delineation of character and to the organization of an adequately unified form, of the best that could be found in Europe. There is nevertheless worthwhile music in operas by Michael Balfe, Edward Loder and Vincent Wallace from the years before 1870. Later, the influence of Wagner and Strauss, as well as of lesser figures like Raff, did not greatly improve the situation, and despite the strengths of both Hamish MacCunn and Delius as opera composers it remains evident that for British opera at its post-Purcellian best we must wait until 1945 and Britten's *Peter Grimes*. Only Ethel Smyth, dated though her stage works soon became, seemed to foreshadow the dramatic virtues of that later style.

Nineteenth-century England was not a fertile breeding-ground for Romantic principles, not least because the new middle class, powerful in economic and political terms, was characterized more by a philistine puritanism than by cultural open-mindedness. It is therefore particularly apt that a composer in whom the tension between middle-class social conventions and what can only be termed a sort of Catholic misanthropy is so strongly represented was the first to create an English late Romanticism of truly international quality. However much credit is given to the precursors of Elgar, from the Weber pupil Julius Benedict to Parry and MacCunn, it was only with Elgar's own early cantatas that the foundations of that Romanticism were well and truly laid. Only then, as Stephen Banfield claims, did English composers join their 'romantic brethren in other countries and other arts in accepting the opposing forces' – artists and society – 'and the inherent alienation' – of the artist in society – 'as a source of creativity'.

Elgar's life can certainly be seen in terms of that 'inherent alienation' inspiring music of unprecedented – for Britain – emotional intensity. Even his partsongs of the 1890s can sound surprisingly uninhibited by comparison with more typical examples of the genre, by such as Parry. Elgar could achieve an altogether more powerful focusing of feeling into form than Parry, Stanford or any of his British contemporaries. As a result, stylistic debts to other composers – Brahms, Strauss – came to count for very little, and his orchestral, choral and chamber music of the two decades from the *Enigma* Variations (completed 1899) to the Piano Quintet (completed 1919) forms one of the most distinguished of all contributions to the Romantic repertoire. Delius, for one, might pour scorn on the various links between the First Symphony and Wagner, Verdi, Mendelssohn and Brahms, but that work has a strength of structure and clarity of focus that Delius himself could never match, save perhaps when his preferred ambivalent fluxes attained that true sense of inevitability which some have found in, for example, the Violin Concerto (1916). Delius was a greater original than Elgar, and the crucial role of Debussy's music in his development distances him more than Elgar from the central techniques of Romanticism, while enabling him to retain that emphasis on pure, immediate feeling which is fundamental to Romanticism's world of expression. There is less ecstasy and sensuality in Elgar, less reflection, less narcissism: instead, an altogether more dynamic response to pain and alienation.

42 Elgar in 1903, the year in which his oratorio *The Apostles* was premièred at the Birmingham Festival. The next ten years saw the completion of most of his major orchestral works.

Moreover, it is a measure of Delius's independence of Romanticism's most vital strands of development that he seems so remote from so much of interest and importance that had happened in his adopted country, France, before the emergence of Debussy.

In the 1830s and '40s, Paris had been the principal centre of musical Romanticism, albeit depending more on its ability to attract foreign masters – Meyerbeer, Liszt, Chopin – than on the recognition of native genius (Berlioz). By the early 1870s, however, that leading role had passed to Vienna, and with Berlioz recently dead and Gounod an exile in England, the leading French composer was the thirty-five-year-old Camille Saint-Saëns (1835–1921). There is therefore a natural logic in the change from the eager embrace of foreign composers before 1850 to the situation after 1870 in which the influence of styles and sources from outside was a crucial force in French musical life. And although the claim that in Paris there was nothing to be heard but performances of non-French operas is undoubtedly a distortion, the tendency to favour an orchestral and operatic repertoire of earlier, and German, music, is clear.

The one home-grown success was Gounod's *Faust*, premièred at the Théâtre Lyrique in 1859. Originally an *opéra comique*, *Faust* soon

43 The garden scene from Gounod's *Faust* in the 1864 Covent Garden production. Giovanni Mario as Faust, Jean-Baptiste Faure as Méphistophélès, and Adelina Patti as Marguerite.

acquired recitatives in place of spoken dialogue, and, later still, a ballet. Similarities between its subject-matter and that of Meyerbeer's *Robert le diable* serve to underline the virtues of Gounod's work, in which the shift away from grand-operatic spectacle promotes a new emphasis on character. Charles Gounod (1818–93) revealed a gift for the musical portrayal of human emotions – especially love – to such effect that *Faust* can be said to give a good indication of what a non-Berliozian French Romanticism might have been like. But there is also a good case for saying that it is far from typical of Gounod himself. He was undoubtedly a master of the small-scale, well-turned, attractive melodic line. But the success of *Faust* encouraged him to indulge in the grandiose musical expression of his religious beliefs. From 1870 until his death in 1893 he laboured principally in the field of oratorio and sacred music, with only an occasional glimpse – as in the *Petite symphonie* for wind (1885) – of the freshness and charm which have proved to be his most enduring qualities.

Despite their consistent and evident Frenchness, both Gounod and Saint-Saëns owed debts to German or Germanic musical sources. In Saint-Saëns's case the influence of Liszt is particularly important, emerging in the Third Piano Concerto and the symphonic poems, especially in the best of these, *Phaëton* and *La jeunesse d'Hercule*. Liszt, acknowledging the compliment, gave the première of Saint-Saëns's opera *Samson et Dalila* in Weimar in 1877: it was not staged in France until 1890. *Samson et Dalila*, with its strong feeling of coherence, is definitely a Romantic opera which has severed links with the separate numbers of *opéra comique*, and although the music cannot match either the eroticism of Wagner or the earthiness of Verdi, it does have its own sensuous appeal. So does the symphonic music, though here, too, comparisons operate to Saint-Saëns's disadvantage. Even in the popular Symphony no. 3 (with organ), first performed in 1886, the attempt at a grand final apotheosis seems overblown alongside Mendelssohn or Schumann, pretentious and thin alongside Bruckner or Mahler. When it aims for serenity, as in the slow movement, the music is bland. At its best, in the first movement and Scherzo, it recalls the restless energy of Tchaikovsky's symphonic music, though without its consistent intensity. In the work as a whole, the fact that expansiveness and opulence are not sufficiently matched by strong symphonic argument and structure suggests that Saint-Saëns was not a natural late Romantic. Sobriety and good humour became him more than flamboyance and rhetoric, and he is most memorable in the unforced lyricism of a work like the late Clarinet Sonata (1921).

Similar reservations about the relevance of 'Romantic' as a label apply to Georges Bizet (1838–75). All agree that *Carmen* was Bizet's masterpiece. Whether it is a *Romantic* masterpiece is much more difficult to say, and many writers, building on the celebrated views of Nietzsche, who found it a refuge from all he had come to detest in Wagner, prefer to stress its Realism. It is not just that *Carmen* is an opera about 'passion' rather than 'romance' – so are *Tristan* and *Otello* – or that its characters are less than heroic, its setting in no way idealized or stylized. In its original form as an *opéra comique* with spoken dialogue, the alternation of speech and music actually serves to reinforce this unstylized realism. Bizet's skill lies precisely in the way he juggles with potentially conflicting extremes and achieves a convincing synthesis. Thus the sheer intensity of feeling, arising from his refusal to glamorize or in any way to dilute the drama, is all the greater because he shuns that shameless indulgence of his characters which later Realists did not always avoid. The characters are more convincing because the composer preserves a degree of detachment; the story is the more impressively realistic because the composer preserves the essential formalities of the *opéra comique* design.

Refusing to soften the impact of tragedy is, presumably, one of the hallmarks of great drama in any style or of any period, and even if *Carmen* is not itself Romantic it had a great impact on the Romantic era, as comments like those of Tchaikovsky quoted earlier (p. 139) – a fusion of fascination and distaste – make clear. After all, however much Bizet may be said to have used Romantic *techniques* – of harmony, in particular – the originality of *Carmen* does lie in its challenge to the more idealistic Romanticism of Liszt and Wagner. It could hardly be otherwise, for Bizet's own attitude to art seems to have been straightforwardly commercial; he was concerned to produce work of good quality of the type that would stand a good chance of success. And so, more directly than any other work of its period, *Carmen* anticipates the authentic *verismo* of Puccini and his contemporaries. Ironically, but not unexpectedly, it had little influence in France, where things Germanic remained more significant until the years of Debussy's maturity.

One cannot imagine anyone seeking to term Bizet 'la fille de Gounod' – the label applied to Massenet – but Bizet and Massenet shared relative freedom alike from the seductions of Wagner and the Franckian sonata-style: even if aspects of *Esclarmonde*, *Manon* and *Werther* can all be related to Wagnerian tendencies, they never for a moment approach the most fundamental aspects of Wagner's style or aesthetic. In what is probably his best work – *Manon* (1884) – Massenet (1842–1912) actually makes a virtue of his limitations, that post-Gounod emphasis on what now seem mildly erotic situations, to produce an efficiently crafted, effective piece of theatre. Tchaikovsky provides an indication of how Massenet seemed to a contemporary. In 1879 he wrote that 'I am quite in love with Massenet's *Le roi de Lahore* . . . I would give a lot for my *Maid of Orleans* to be as good'; five years later, however, he commented that 'I expected more from *Manon Lescaut* [sic] . . . Massenet himself was not up to the mark. He is beginning to get colourless, and boring, in spite of much effect and very fine work from beginning to end.' Although enough of an opportunist not to reject all awareness of current developments in both Germany and Russia, Massenet was in essence a master of the superficially attractive rather than a seeker after mystic or mythological profundities. It was therefore entirely appropriate that he should have worked, in his 'drames lyriques', on a smaller scale than that embraced by the more epic qualities of the now defunct grand opera. For all that, his fusion of religious and erotic feeling (deriving from Gounod) is an authentically Romantic one – if of a rather sentimental variety.

A second respect in which Massenet made an impact on French musical life was as professor of composition at the Paris Conservatoire (1878–96). The other great influence of this period, as teacher and composer, was Belgian-born César Franck (1822–90), who, like Saint-Saëns, was much affected by non-French music – Beethoven, Schumann, Liszt. Indeed, Franck's slow growth to maturity – the Piano Quintet of 1879, completed when he was fifty-seven, is generally seen as his first completely characteristic piece – is best explained in terms of the slow and uncertain reaction to personalities stronger than his own; in addition, his limitations are usually ascribed to his inability to absorb the influences of such as Bach, Beethoven and Liszt into a new, individual synthesis, as well as to a devotion to the cosy security of the organ loft. What enabled Franck to rise above such apparently crippling drawbacks was his awareness that the traditional symphonic forms could provide him with a very real and very strong expressive purpose. Even if he wished to, he never succeeded in suppressing that sense of nervous tension that comes from the conscious effort to be worthy of the greatness of the past, and so it is not difficult to relate Franck's music to the mainstream of the Romantic struggle with the symphonic, that heroic attempt to adapt anged conditions without totally betraying the Beethovenian ideals. Franck was certainly not afraid to aim at forthright intensity of expression, and the emotional power of, for example, the slow movement of the Piano Quintet is representative of his tendency to look more to Germany than France for spiritual sustenance.

The year of the quintet – 1879 – was also the year in which one of Franck's pupils, Henri Duparc, and Duparc's friend Emmanuel Chabrier attended the performance of *Tristan* in Munich which led to Chabrier's abandonment of his civil service career. (Three years earlier, the first Bayreuth Festival had been attended by Vincent d'Indy (1851–1931); the most dedicated of all Franck's disciples.) The story of Wagner's impact in France, on works like Lalo's *Le roi d'Ys*, Chabrier's *Gwendoline* and *Le roi malgré lui*, has often been told, and whatever virtues one may discover in these works it is surely the case that the French Wagnerians were at their best when least directly imitating, if not when positively reacting against, the Magician of Bayreuth. Significantly, perhaps, Franck himself never visited the Festspielhaus; and although his encounter with the Prelude to *Tristan* in 1874 had its effect on his harmony, an even deeper allegiance went to the composer whose music might in the 1880s have been felt to be less complete, and to contain more genuine potential for development, especially with respect to cyclic symphonic procedures – Franz Liszt. It was between 1880 and 1890 that Franck produced his own major instrumental pieces, including the symphonic poems *Le chasseur maudit* and *Les djinns*, the string quartet, the violin sonata, and the symphony, all genuinely late Romantic in their eager embrace of direct emotional expression. Their strengths, as Debussy was to note in respect of the symphony, were in their melodic ideas and their emotional power. Their weakness was a tendency to excessively foursquare phrase structure, though the kind of formal flexibility found perhaps most persuasively in the strongly organic, cyclic elements of the violin sonata can compensate for this. At his best, Franck is a distinctive, even arresting composer whose expressiveness seems the more effective for his evident distrust of the grander rhetoric of the Wagnerians – even though, of course, close study of Wagner might have cured that 'foursquare phrase structure'!

By the time of Franck's death, in 1890, Wagner's musical influence had passed its peak, but the impact of his ideas – his 'philosophy' – continued to be strong. The founding of the Schola Cantorum by d'Indy, Guilmant and Bordes in 1894, with its emphasis on sacred music, might therefore have been expected to reflect a growing anti-Bayreuth and anti-Romantic reaction. Nevertheless, composition itself continued to reflect the resilience of things Wagnerian. D'Indy had initially been more strongly influenced by Liszt, and although in the 1890s a 'nationalist' streak becomes evident in his use of the folk music from the Vivarais district, the Wagner influence was still to assert itself fully. D'Indy enshrines a characteristic French conflict; for although his strongest commitment was to notions of Classicism he saw no contradiction between these notions and musical practices directly stemming from German late Romanticism. As early as 1876 he condemned *Aida* as a 'Meyerbeerian-Wagneroid bore', yet in 1897 he produced *Fervaal*, an opera whose fidelity to Wagnerian precepts may have ensured its modernity but does little to bring that modernity to life: it is certainly a good deal more boring than *Aida*, if owing less to Meyerbeer. D'Indy's later opera *L'étranger* (1901) is another exploration of Wagnerian ideas, and fails to improve on its predecessor. But his later orchestral works are more rewarding: in particular, the symphonic poem *Jour d'été à la montagne* (1905), which shows the French Lisztian inheritance nearing its end, but still – defiantly – alive.

Several other French composers – Alkan, Chausson, Duparc, Lekeu – are better termed 'Romantic' than anything else – not least the short-lived Lekeu, with his particular concern to use Beethoven's later style as his model and ideal. Duparc's few, fine songs are if anything closer to Liszt and Wagner in harmonic technique than to Franck. But the most significant creative minds apart from Massenet and Franck active at this time were Fauré (1845–1924) and, in the 1890s, Debussy. In his consistent avoidance of rhetoric Fauré was, at best, a Romantic after the model of Chopin or Schumann, while in his enriched tonal vocabulary Romantic techniques advance towards a more radical Impressionism. Debussy (1862–1918), with his early affinity for Russian rather than German Romanticism, was nevertheless even more hostile than Fauré to overstatement. The anti-Wagnerianism of *Pelléas et Mélisande* is hardly anti-Romanticism, as the love music makes clear, and yet Debussy's progressiveness, linking him more directly with twentieth-century radicals, is such as to make it both implausible and anachronistic to seek to attach him at all firmly to Romantic traditions after the mid-1890s. Of his contemporaries, Paul Dukas (1865–1935) is a more convincing candidate for such attachment, not least because rhetoric is not banished from his opera *Ariane et Barbe-bleu* (1907): and Wagner, Liszt and Richard Strauss (as well as Franck) all come to mind at times in Dukas's instrumental and orchestral music. Nevertheless, the French composer of the early twentieth century who was closest to the essential qualities of late Romanticism was Florent Schmitt (1870–1958), at least in a work like the ballet *La tragédie de Salomé* (1907), where associations with both Strauss and Rimsky-Korsakov underline its powerful eroticism.

Romanticism in America certainly extends well beyond the fringe in the sense that the most prominent American composers of the first half of the nineteenth century – A. P. Heinrich (1781–1861) and L. M. Gottschalk (1829–69) – were both much more than pale or even robust shadows of their European contemporaries. Heinrich's *Grand American Chivalrous Symphony* and Gottschalk's Symphony no. 1, *La nuit des tropiques*, immediately indicate the importance of national, or at least non-European themes, and the self-taught Heinrich and the Paris-trained Gottschalk were both nationalists as much as Romantics. Nevertheless, the originality and eccentricity of this generation of composers did not universally commend itself, and an important strain in American late Romanticism, best represented by Edward MacDowell (1860–1908) and J. K. Paine (1839–1906), sought more orthodox instruction in Germany and then put that instruction into practice in well-made symphonic works and programmatic pieces. Charles T. Griffes (1884–1920), a pupil of Humperdinck, is the composer who most notably enshrines an evolution from Germanic late Romanticism to something more progressive, while other early twentieth-century composers unashamedly used American folk materials in the service of European styles: Henry Gilbert's use of Creole tunes in his symphonic poem *The Dance in the Place Congo*, the style recalling Tchaikovsky or Grieg, and John Powell's employment of black American materials in his *Rhapsodie nègre* after the manner of Liszt are the most frequently cited examples – neither exactly familiar outside works of reference. But the greatest and best-known American late Romantic, to the extent that he fails to escape all such categorization, is Charles Ives (1874–1954), whose most substantial works – like the *Concord* Piano Sonata and the Symphony no. 4 – turn a fascination with transcendentalism entirely representative of the American Romantic tradition to remarkably radical, forward-looking and even post-Romantic ends.

CHAPTER ELEVEN

Symphony and song:
Vienna in the later nineteenth century

Wagner was the great Romantic specialist, the creative force who transformed the medium of opera and confined himself entirely to the new world of music drama that resulted. In their tendency to choose symphony rather than opera as their preferred form of expression, the other later German Romantics were also specialists of a kind, but specialists with a far greater potential for displaying anti-Romantic traits, while also – rather paradoxically – having in at least one case – Brahms – been much closer to one of the earlier Romantics than Wagner ever was. Brahms (1833–97) first met Schumann in 1853; he was close to the family for the remaining three years of Schumann's life; and his subsequent relationship with Clara was clearly crucial, though its nature remains tantalizingly obscure.

Wagner was also special in that – regally – he expected audiences to attend his court. Brahms was most closely associated with a very different environment, Vienna: he moved to the Austrian capital at the age of twenty-nine in 1862, settled there permanently in 1868, and contributed notably to the resurgence of the city's musical life. 'Resurgence' is an appropriate term because, despite its relatively rich operatic and concert life, no truly great composer was resident in Vienna between the late 1820s and the late 1860s. Moreover, the occasional contacts of Schumann, Berlioz, Liszt and Wagner with the city were not always rewarding. After a visit in 1878 Wagner wrote to the Opera Director that 'when I parted from you . . . I was certain that I would never enter Vienna again. There every scoundrelly dog can fall on a man like me . . . but, thank goodness, I need never show my face there again. Never! Never!' Such heated reactions make it easier to explain Brahms's evident liking for the city in terms of a shared conservatism which affected, though by no means eliminated, Romantic musical qualities. With the building of the new opera house (it opened in May 1869 not with a new work but with *Don Giovanni* in German), the establishment during the 1860s of the regular seasons of Philharmonic Orchestral Concerts (which have

44 The music room in Brahms's Viennese apartment. The portrait on the far left is of Cherubini. On the right, a relief portrait of Bismarck and a bust of Beethoven.

taken place ever since 1870 in the Grosser Musikvereinssaal) and, not least, the emergence of Viennese operetta with Suppé's *Flotte Bursche* (1863), the foundations were laid for that fruitful tension between conservative and radical, lighthearted and intensely serious, that reached its peak in the Expressionist art of the early twentieth century. And it may well be that these conflicts were prefigured in Brahms himself, by a productive confrontation between Romantic expressiveness and conservative, Classical order.

Such a view risks oversimplification, not least because it leaves out of account the vital effect of pre-Classical music on Brahms's development. Indeed, Brahms can be seen as the greatest of all nineteenth-century 'synthesizers' in his brilliant, resourceful fusion of Baroque counterpoint, Classical symphonism and Romantic expressive immediacy – a fusion that could scarcely have been achieved through conscious intent and clearly owes more to an unusual breadth of musical sympathy (and even a curiosity found most commonly in later times in musicologists rather than in composers) than to any belief that contemporary music itself was

164

either too radical or too narrow. This view of Brahms is all the more persuasive since it need not invalidate the critical response – expressed most extremely and entertainingly by Hugo Wolf in the mid-1880s – that the mixture does not always work: the music can seem pedestrian, overloaded, lacking in spontaneity, not just in comparison with the avatars of 'New German' innovation (Wagner, Liszt) but in comparison with Brahms himself at his (normal) best. Nor does this interpretation of Brahms the composer conflict with a view of Brahms the man as beset by the tension between strictness and freedom, a man essentially insecure and reluctant to embark on emotional commitments. The banality of such characterizations does not for a moment prevent them from being true, of course, and the only thing that makes them of interest – since they are scarcely unusual – is their connection with a man who wrote great music. The problem with attempts to demythologize the conflicts and tensions of Brahms's life is that they may make it more difficult to present a convincing case for his essential Romanticism. Not for the first time in this present narrative, that case may find itself in danger of being accused not of inaccuracy so much as of irrelevance. After all, at least when matters of technique are under discussion, it is nowadays not Brahms's Romanticism but his progressiveness which is stressed.

The stimulus for this orientation is Schoenberg's celebrated essay 'Brahms the Progressive', with all its tantalizing loose ends, and the invitation it extends to see Brahms not in opposition to Liszt and Wagner but as revealing comparable concerns, with respect to harmony and thematic processes, if not to form as such. From this angle, differences of style and range of influences, or sources, matter less than the common – Romantic – awareness of those aspects of the post-Beethovenian musical language that possessed the greatest potential, whether the medium was symphony or music drama, string quartet or tone poem. And it is in their shared attitudes to ways of extending tonality and rethinking the regular phrase-structure of Classical tradition that Brahms, Liszt and Wagner can be shown to make common cause, and to offer conclusive evidence of responses and procedures decisively distant from anything that could be termed Classical – or even Neoclassical.

It is right that Brahms, of all composers, should continue to provoke this kind of debate. After all, if there is such a thing as a 'Romantic' musical language, as distinct from Romantic styles and subjects, it is one richer in chromatic inflection and phrase-structural and formal diversity than the Classical language that preceded it. The essential synthesis in Brahms is that between the 'foreground' of at times turbulent, at times elevated expressiveness achieved by the 'progressive' harmonic and thematic processes noted above, and the Classically-derived formal principles, promoting unities of a kind quite remote from the freer, if still (for the most part) organically evolving schemes of Liszt or Wagner. The 'foreground' is Romantic, the 'background' Classical; and Brahms was a Romantic because the unique expressive qualities and techniques which could have existed at no other time were themselves moulded and enriched by a range of Classical – and Baroque – models and influences. These qualities span his entire career, from the explosive and reflective extremes of the early piano sonatas and the First Piano Concerto (1854–8) to the dramatic concentration and cogent vigour of the Fourth Symphony (1883) and Double Concerto (1887) and on to the more richly reflective yet never loosely structured or mawkish Clarinet Quintet and sonatas (1891–4). Much of the vigour in Brahms's music is due to his predilection for 'folklike' (at times Hungarian) material. But his mastery is evident alike in the quiet miniatures (some of the songs and the sets of piano pieces, especially opp. 118 and 119 of 1892) and in the large-scale orchestral and chamber works on which his reputation of handing down the Classical forms to the twentieth century – and of being the first nineteenth-century composer of symphonic music to measure up to the challenge of Beethoven – rests.

The aspect of Brahms's character that probably seems most remote from modern modes of thought is the kind of secular Christianity which prompted the non-liturgical but emphatically Biblical German Requiem and gives the Four Serious Songs their unrivalled gravity and sense of strict, human morality. A Bible-reading devotee of Bismarck who had much experience of human weaknesses (from the onset of Schumann's madness to the breakdown of his parents' marriage), Brahms was clearly more concerned with ways of living life on earth most effectively than with preparing for a possible after-life. After all, Brahms was one of the first musicians to sense just how greatly contemporary life could be enriched not by listening to old music alone but by exploring its sources: it has even been claimed (by J. Peter Burkholder) that in thus establishing the one essential challenge of twentieth-century music – how to achieve a creative

45 Brahms in his later years. The 'Bible-reading devotee of Bismarck' was by no means a totally austere figure.

synthesis of old and new – Brahms ought to be held as more significant today than Wagner, for whom the old was, ultimately, of little account. Here, perhaps, lies that integration of progressiveness with genuine success (both artistically and with the public) that makes Brahms such a formidable and fascinating presence in the 'Romantic Century'.

If Anton Bruckner (1824–96) is to be regarded as a less 'successful' symphonic composer than Brahms – a big 'if', admittedly – the argument might be that he was not merely more enthusiastic about Wagner but also more of a true Romantic. By contrast, most recent writers on Bruckner have sought to stress his uniqueness, and to regard any attempts to associate him at all significantly with the temper of the times as dubious, if not counter-productive. Thus, his use of sonata form has been strongly contrasted with more traditional, conventional schemes in which a single, dynamic progress to a goal keeps all tendencies to contrast and conflict subordinate, and the separate movements of his symphonies have not been seen as building towards a finale that necessarily sums up the whole work in authentically Romantic, organic fashion.

In view of Bruckner's well-nigh notorious liking for making strong breaks between the stages of his separate symphonic movements, it might seem quite acceptable to regard him as representing that concern with parts rather than wholes which, this study argues, is no less 'Romantic' in essence than ultra-organic integration and unity. Nevertheless, there is surely a case to be made for the argument that Bruckner's symphonic blocks do ultimately enhance large-scale, underlying continuity; and even critics whose short-term chordal view of harmony prevents them from doing justice to the larger linearities of Bruckner's tonal schemes ought to find it difficult to deny to the overwhelming perorations of Bruckner's greatest finales – those of the Fifth and Eighth Symphonies – their function as the crowning resolution of the entire, gigantic edifice. They are too grand, too exalted, to be the goal of the finale alone. And while Deryck Cooke is quite right to say that Bruckner's 'new and monumental type of symphonic organicism' abjures alike 'the terse, dynamic continuity of Beethoven, and the broad, fluid continuity of Wagner', it is less clear that what Cooke terms the 'elemental and metaphysical' qualities which Bruckner's music expresses are totally unrelated to such qualities in Beethoven and Wagner respectively. Bruckner was certainly a great original, and his greatness ensures that his originality is not compromised by associations with other composers in particular, or with Romanticism in general.

Cooke does admit to finding a 'Romantic grandeur' in the D minor and F minor Masses (1864, 1866), works that came into being in circumstances very different from those with which most of the great Romantic masters would have been content. Bruckner (1824–96), one of the slowest of slow developers, was, in Cooke's memorable phrase, 'a simple and pious villager who unwillingly became a controversial figure in a big city' – that same city where Brahms so willingly lived and worked. Not until 1868, when he was forty-four, did Bruckner finally settle in Vienna, and begin to put his lengthy apprenticeship (culminating in lessons by correspondence with Simon Sechter) to use. That apprenticeship seems a spectacularly neurotic manifestation in one who was himself a teacher, though teachers are not always the most reluctant of all professionals to continue their own education. But even Bruckner's insecurity is difficult to interpret. It seems likely that both his various obsessions and his deep uncertainty about his compositions were, in a sense, neurotic in origin: the essentially secretive stubbornness of the numeromaniac is perhaps not inconsistent with the cast of mind which acted on suggestions for revisions of the symphonies while preserving his private faith in his 'definitively complete scores' – a phrase with which Cooke indicates the complex editorial problems created by the various versions of those works. Bruckner, claims Cooke, 'regarded unauthentic revisions as makeshifts, useful only in that they suited the taste of his own time.'

He was certainly not the kind of person to expect much from that time, and his personality must have been deeply affected by tension between an apparently unshakable religious faith and his efforts to live a secular life. That life, despite the embarrassments of his approaches to women and a good deal of critical hostility, was not without success. He acquired a group of devoted pupils, and did eventually receive a degree of acclaim for his symphonies, if more outside Vienna than within it. For the iconoclastic young Hugo Wolf, Bruckner – though not allowed to go uncriticized – was 'a Titan in conflict with the gods'. The more common view – that of Brahms, for one – was that his works were 'symphonic boa-constrictors'. Of course, the differences between the two great symphonists were profound, and it seems simplistic today to attribute those differences solely, or even principally to Wagner, though he was undoubtedly an important factor. Brahms tended to avoid the

46 Bruckner in 1894. Two years before his death, he was at work on his 9th Symphony, destined to remain unfinished.

47 Hugo Wolf, the haunted master of the late Romantic Lied.

'Epic' tone. His symphonies and concertos may have powerful, even heroic climaxes, but the economical nature of his materials and forms gives his music the kind of dynamic concentration and continuity that relates more directly to Beethoven and the other Classical masters than does anything in Bruckner. By contrast, Bruckner, the disciple of Schubert, is at his best when his expansiveness is most powerfully sustained, bridging the structural gaps and contrasts which are such prominent surface features. And Bruckner was particularly successful in his slow movements, which have a tone of exalted serenity foreign to Brahms. Above all, Bruckner had the naivety necessary to profit from the 'Epic' tone of Wagner. In Cooke's diagnosis, the expanded time-scale, slow-moving harmonies, use of full brass and intense string cantabile all stem from Wagner. But Bruckner made them his own, just as he transformed the four-movement model of Beethoven and Schubert into a scheme in which the episodic stimulates and ultimately reinforces the organic. Bruckner's single movements by no means always achieve the totally satisfying proportions, the absolute sense of inevitable balance of detail and totality, of the best of Brahms. But the sense of awe and elation conveyed by a movement like the Adagio of the Eighth Symphony – awe in face of resplendent divinity, elation in realization of humanity at its most noble – is unique and as powerful as anything in music.

Writing of Bruckner's Seventh Symphony in 1886, Hugo Wolf (1860–1903) remarked that the composer 'has not been spared the age-old painful experience of the prophet without honour in his own land. Struggling for decades in vain against the obtuseness and hostility of critics, rejected by the concert institutions, pursued by envy and ill-will, he was already an old man when fortune kissed his brow and the thankless world pressed laurel wreaths upon his head. Not even Berlioz had so bad a time of it as Bruckner.' Whether or not Wolf himself consciously rejected the possibility of such an heroic life of suffering, he made only very intermittent attempts – through the symphonic poem as a young man, and opera later on – to compose on that large scale which seemed the necessary, inevitable task for the disciple of Berlioz, Liszt and Wagner, and the admirer of Bruckner. Wolf may simply have lacked the gift for sustained creative work: of his more than two hundred songs, the vast majority were written within about eighteen months of, in total, a nine-year period (1888–97). From his childhood it was clear that music alone mattered to him, yet, without the willingness or ability to work as a teacher, he needed the opportunities for patronage and casual work (such as journalism) which only a large city like Vienna could provide. Moreover, he acquired, in about 1878, when he was eighteen, a syphilitic infection which stimulated creativity for short periods and also acted as a permanent, frightening *memento mori*. It is therefore scarcely surprising that creative work was only intermittently possible, and that the music itself, at its finest, should represent a powerful, positive confrontation: between relatively small-scale forms and the origins, in much larger musical dimensions, of Wolf's style and techniques. It may strain credulity to regard Wolf's Lieder as the purest distillation of Wagnerian music drama, Lisztian tone poem and Brucknerian symphony, yet in the tendency to give the piano part a self-contained, flexibly structured thematic/harmonic argument of the kind which served the expressive essence of the text most graphically, and to place the vocal setting of the text itself with maximum attention to qualities of word–tone synthesis rather than pure melody, Wolf did indeed achieve a remarkable focusing of all that was most essential in the various symphonic dramas (with or without texts) of his models.

It might seem, from this, that Wolf could be the ultimate musical Romantic, refining the essence of all that was grandest and most radical in nineteenth-century music into statements from which all inflation and exaggeration had been purged. It is therefore worth pointing out at once how much comedy, serenity and sheer happiness there is in Wolf's Lieder. If the purest Romanticism is in the melancholy moods of lost love and isolation in nature, or in man's defiance in the face of personal tragedy or natural disaster, then Wolf is by no means exclusively preoccupied with such matters, especially in those settings of Eichendorff peopled by a variety of picaresque individuals from soldiers to musicians – a character which also informs the lighter items of the Spanish and Italian Song Books. It also does less than justice to Wolf's originality to stress his Lisztian, Wagnerian or Brucknerian heritage at the expense of other factors; for example, his debt to Schumann, which has little to do with style as such, but is evident in his tendency to group songs into 'books' and the prominence of his piano accompaniments.

Moreover, when it comes to 'refining the essence' of Wagnerian music drama, it seems undeniable that, in the all-important relation between words and music, Wolf was closer to Wagner's theories of word-tone synthesis, as expressed in *Opera and Drama*, than to his practice in the music dramas themselves. There is a necessary imbalance in Wagner's later dramas between words and music – necessary because of the long-term structural goals which only the symphonic structuring of the orchestral music can adequately embody. But only very rarely does one of Wolf's songs give such emphasis to non-vocal music as that most musico-dramatic of them all, the setting of Goethe's *Prometheus*. Otherwise, even those songs in which the piano part is most 'symphonic' in its thematic elaboration, like *Auf einer Wanderung* and *Im Frühling*, do not wholly resort to 'musical prose' – a consistent deviation from periodic structure – after the model of the later Wagner. Wolf's recognition of the constraints of – often great – poetry (so different in structure as well as purely literary quality from a Wagner text) might also help to account for a further well-nigh 'anti-Romantic' trait in him: the tendency to function more as observer of, than participant in, the events and feelings so graphically yet sensitively represented. Yet it sells the power of Wolf's expressiveness short to imply that an observer cannot at the same time be deeply involved if not actively participating in the emotional situation: and the detachment that can be read into, for example, Wolf's setting of Goethe's *Anakreons Grab* is surely an expressiveness the more effective (given the song's brevity) for its restraint: but it is restraint, and not detachment, which is of the essence, an ability to understate in the face of great feeling rather than to remove oneself from feeling and in some sense comment on it from outside.

It is certainly difficult to exaggerate the wide range of moods Wolf so brilliantly captures. If Goethe's *Prometheus* represents one extreme – the heroic defiance demanding a much more overtly 'Wagnerian' rhetoric than Wolf normally employed – Mörike's *Im Frühling* embodies another: the recollection, regretful rather than bitter, of past, lost happiness. Wolf's hymns to nature (*Um Mitternacht*, *Fussreise*) are generally as positive as his love songs are impassioned, serene or wry. He is at his most technically progressive in the tortured religious songs of the Spanish Song Book, but he is never more authentically late Romantic than when challenging, and outdoing, Schubert's settings of Goethe. In Wolf's hands, even more than in Schubert's, the figure of the 'Harfenspieler' from *Wilhelm Meister* becomes more than an eccentric minstrel: he seems to embody in concentrated form all that is most anguished and self-aware in the Romantic artist – the isolation, the self-doubt, the need to exploit the resources of music to extract the maximum intensity from them that is consistent with the preservation of ultimate harmonic coherence. These songs are among the greatest monuments of musical Romanticism.

CHAPTER TWELVE

Into the twentieth century

In 1888, Tchaikovsky referred sarcastically to 'the new German genius. Von Bülow fusses over him as he did over Brahms and others. In my opinion there has never yet been anyone of less talent and so full of pretension.' The 'genius' in question was Richard Strauss (1864–1949), whose early compositions aroused no more enthusiasm in a senior critic nearer home. In 1892, Hanslick reacted strongly against the symphonic poem *Don Juan*: 'The tragedy is that most of our younger composers think in a foreign language (philosophy, poetry, painting) and then translate the thought into the mother tongue (music). People like Richard Strauss, moreover, translate badly, unintelligibly, tastelessly, with exaggeration.' And the following year, hearing *Tod und Verklärung*, Hanslick concluded that it belonged, 'with *Don Juan*, among the products of over-cultivation in our music . . . The basic characteristic of Strauss as a symphonist is that he composes with poetic rather than with musical elements and, through his emancipation from musical logic, takes a position rather adjacent to music than squarely in it.'

By the end of his career, Hanslick was thoroughly saddened by the persistence of those more radical strains of Romanticism that he had devoted so much time to condemning. In 1894 he wearily singled out Humperdinck as cleverly matching the 'spirit of the time. The public desires new themes and yet adheres to Wagnerism. Humperdinck [in *Hänsel und Gretel*] satisfied both requirements.' And the old campaigner allowed himself one final, waspish sting, noting Siegfried Wagner's claim that *Hänsel und Gretel* was 'the most important opera since *Parsifal*. In other words, the best in a full twelve years? An irritating pronouncement, and the worst of it is – that it is true.'

Where musicians a century after Hanslick may find themselves agreeing with the tone of his remarks is in his ardent belief not simply that the present was inferior to the past but that music had taken a turn after Wagner and Liszt (and, as would soon be the case, after Brahms too) from which only a truly radical rethinking of essentially *musical*

48 The young Richard Strauss.
An essentially conservative yet
endlessly resourceful late
Romantic.

factors could save it. And although one can hardly feel confident that
Hanslick would have approved of the work of Debussy, Bartók,
Stravinsky, Schoenberg and the other great creators of modern
music, it was their achievement to compose on the basis of new kinds
of musical logic (some of which it is still easier to sense than to define
with technical precision). And yet perhaps the most fundamental of all
the general features of twentieth-century music is that the essentially
new has never driven out the essentially old. It is under the heading of
'essentially old' that the survival (often surprisingly vigorous and
resourceful) of Romanticism belongs: and no figure is more
representative of the power and distinction of that survival than
Hanslick's much-despised Richard Strauss.

   To see Strauss accused of an 'emancipation from musical logic'
may bring a wry smile to the lips of those for whom his particular
brand of unregenerate Romanticism (allowing, of course, for the
impressive but soon corrected lurch into Expressionism in *Elektra*) is
confirmation of his fundamentally conservative instincts and
attitudes. Strauss remained a Romantic because he took fright at the
prospect of atonality, and although he encouraged the young
Schoenberg he consciously distanced himself from the implications of

that firebrand's 'emancipation of the dissonance' – a notion much more deserving, it would seem, of Hanslick's barb about 'logic'. True, there is often a note-spinning garrulousness about Strauss's later work – particularly evident in the autobiographical *jeu d'esprit, Intermezzo* (completed 1923) – which the unsympathetic can conveniently equate with potential if not actual senile babble. But at its best Strauss's preservation of the technical principles and expressive qualities of Romanticism has a strength and an individuality which only the most crabbed in spirit can resist. From the sublime simplicities of the final stages of *Der Rosenkavalier* (completed 1910) through to the touching, poised yet never posturing final cadences of the best works of the 1940s – *Capriccio*, the Four Last Songs – the depth of true feeling ensures that even trivial, in-turned, lighthearted moods and situations are transformed in supremely memorable and affecting fashion. And there is much more to this latterday Romanticism than warmed-over sentiment and nostalgia. Technically, Strauss shows the skill of a master in sensing precisely how far his tonal chords and progressions can be coloured and elaborated without becoming impotent and aimless. And this is because he never wholly lost the epic force of the large-scale thinking that makes *Salome*, *Elektra* and, above all, *Die Frau ohne Schatten* compelling musical, as well as dramatic, experiences.

49 Mahler in 1902, the year of his marriage to Alma Schindler, and the completion of his 5th Symphony.

The pairing of Strauss and Gustav Mahler (1860–1911) immediately generates those bold comparisons so helpful to summary accounts. Strauss, also a fine conductor but long-lived, not basically a symphonist, more a traditionalist – the elements of contrast and similarity are obvious. Mahler's influence (or at least the declared admiration of younger and later composers from Schoenberg and Berg to Henze and Maxwell Davies) may frequently be detected as a source of some of the twentieth century's most powerful music – music whose radical, primarily non-tonal language severs it from the fount of nineteenth-century Romanticism, yet which may still be experienced as an intensification – Expressionist or otherwise – of that essentially Romantic atmosphere. (In addition, a strong Mahlerian influence is evident in two of the century's most appealing post-Romantics, Britten and Shostakovich.) Exactly how such diverse 'pupils' relate to the master's own personal achievement is an interesting and (surprisingly) unstudied question. Yet those aspects of style and technique that have influenced later composers have not, on the whole, led to attempts to 'out-Mahler' Mahler. Particular large-scale works (from Schoenberg's *Gurrelieder* to Maxwell Davies's *Worldes Blis*) may set new standards for the elaboration of their vocal and orchestral textures, or the intensity of their symphonic processes. But Mahler's own oeuvre – the ten symphonies, with *Das Lied von der Erde* and the various smaller-scale song collections – has an integrity which even those later composers (Shostakovich, Henze) who have more than matched it in bulk have not – so far – transcended in spirit.

Mahler's late Romanticism may be defined as a structural expansion integrated with an expressive intensification of the symphonic form as handed down from Beethoven through Schubert to Bruckner. The dangers of viewing Mahler's symphonies as somehow the direct result of enthusiasm for Bruckner (and hostility to Brahms) have been rightly stressed in the Mahler literature. Listeners are more likely to be struck by differences in atmosphere than by any similarities of form, and one major difference, from Bruckner and from Brahms alike, is that it might often seem that Mahler (to quote Hanslick once again) 'composes with poetic rather than with musical elements'. Even if the intensity of feeling common to Mahler's symphonies proves that they are the works of a composer who simply did not dare to attempt a 'proper' music drama, however, it must surely be conceded that this intensity would dissipate in undirected gesticulation were it not for the presence of powerfully effective structures. Strength and effectiveness are not, however, to be equated with the presence of traditional symphonic schemes. Mahler's genius lay less in the invention of distinguished thematic ideas (he was often content with very basic melodic patterns whose continuations could come close to the purest banality) than in the creation of the harmonic and formal designs best suited to their statement, elaboration, confrontation and apotheosis. For many, his slow movements (especially the slow finales of the Third and Ninth Symphonies and *Das Lied*) reveal him at his greatest, even if the full power of his faster, more dynamic structures is also acknowledged – often at their most impressive when reacting to the archetype of the military march, as in the first movement of the Sixth Symphony. The 'Romantic' defiance of such music, the fist shaken at fate, is doubtless more inspiriting than the resignation, however serene, of the slow movements – but when, as in the finales of the Ninth and *Das Lied*, there is a breakthrough from despair to acceptance, then the music becomes inspiring as well as memorable.

It may nevertheless be that the explicit poetic content of the finale of *Das Lied von der Erde* helps to make this the most directly and deeply expressive of all Mahler's works. In particular, the breakthrough at the very end to a vision of a new world grounded in positive feelings is a match for the idealized optimism that seems to surface at the very end of the *Ring*. Such optimism, with its apparently unqualified idealism, may seem all the more poignant to a later, less sanguine age. But *Das Lied von der Erde* is also something of a structural miracle, the flexible coherence of its balancing, contrasted movements and immensely wide range of moods and textures a testimonial to all that ideals of progressiveness had been working towards throughout the Romantic century. It is, precisely, more balanced than organic, more coherent than unified. And while some Mahlerians may always marginally prefer to identify and admire the more explicit remodellings of symphonic traditions in the Eighth and Ninth symphonies, in particular, it is difficult not to feel that the actual level of invention in *Das Lied* is consistently higher than in any of the numbered symphonies.

Not least because he has provided concert-promoting and record-making organizations with a repertoire that has proved commercially successful, Mahler has become a central figure of musical late

Romanticism. Giacomo Puccini (1858–1924) is another, and if he (undeniably a great commercial success in the opera house) is less readily identified with late Romanticism than Mahler it is because the ideals attaching to this label may not always seem to fit comfortably with the more overt decadence and, it may be, opportunism of the Italian. Compared (as he often is) with Verdi, Puccini inevitably seems more neurotic, a pampered bourgeois rather than a national hero active in politics, less interested in robust family tensions and honest passions as dramatic themes than in mere sentiment, or more suggestive and sordid sexual topics. At its best, all this may be seen as a justifiable intensification of Romanticism's obsession with the irrational as something which can serve to give humanity a healthy sense of its own weaknesses and limitations: at worst, it is a sad reflection of the unhealthy preoccupations of the *fin de siècle*, in which art loses all capacity to elevate and ennoble, and when it may even lack the will to break out of the late Romantic impasse into a world of courageous and radical experimentation.

While there is no doubt a strong element of the opportunistic about the products of post-Verdian operatic *verismo* in Italy (and elsewhere) it will not do to pigeon-hole Puccini himself as nothing more than a calculating, cynical purveyor of operatic kitsch and soft pornography. His earlier operas are close to pure Romanticism – notably the uneven but in the end genuinely tragic *Manon Lescaut* (1893) and, of course, *La Bohème* (1896); and even during his most 'decadent' period, with the 'Realist' works, *Tosca*, *Madama Butterfly* and *La fanciulla del West* (1900–10), he not only towered above even the best of his veristic rivals (Mascagni, Leoncavallo, Giordano) but confirmed that he possessed the instincts and techniques of a true musical dramatist, irrespective of the types of subject chosen for his works.

The adumbration of Realism in such operas as *La traviata* and *Carmen*, and the more precise preparation of the full-blooded veristic style (which can be linked to a transmutation of certain Wagnerian devices as they pass through the powerful musical fabric of Verdi's *Otello*) promoted an art which – in Mascagni's *Cavalleria rusticana* (1890) and Leoncavallo's *Pagliacci* (1892) – encouraged the crude exaggeration of what, in melodrama, is already larger than life, into the most inflated emotional posturing. Such indulgence is never the whole story in Puccini (save possibly in *Tosca*), not least because he never wholly lost his feeling for the more refined – or at any rate less

50 Poster for Puccini's opera *La fanciulla del West*, issued by his publishers in 1910.

barnstorming – music of such French composers as Gounod, Thomas and Massenet. And for all his evident melodic opulence and readiness to unleash stirring climaxes, Puccini is perhaps most memorable in moments of relative restraint, like the Humming Chorus in *Madama Butterfly* or the delicate – again wordless – waltz tune from *La fanciulla del West*. And it is his capacity for keeping the tendency to excess and crudity at bay that makes Puccini a true heir, and continuer, of genuine Romanticism. This Romanticism – as in the pathos of Mimi's death – has nothing to do with the irruption of irrational and dark forces (indeed, it is often said that the opera romanticizes the heroine of Murger's novel out of all recognition); and the same sense of genuine pathos is evident in *Butterfly*, which, coming after the blood-and-thunder of *Tosca*, seems much more tender than decadent, and is 'veristic' without ever indulging in effects for their own sake.

Passion without profundity, the sensuous at the expense of the spiritual, continue to inform Puccini's most characteristic later works from *La fanciulla* to *Turandot*. He was sufficiently touched by progressiveness to reflect the more radical harmonic developments of the years after 1910, and even found something not utterly negative to say about Schoenberg in the last year of his life. To this extent, therefore, Puccini became a more equivocal late Romantic than Rakhmaninov, the only other twentieth-century composer to rival him in the sheer popularity of at least some of his music.

Sergei Rakhmaninov (1874–1943) may not be the last Russian Romantic – such an ascription is especially difficult in a country where stylistic conservatism remains a pressing social obligation – but he must be accounted one of the most consistent twentieth-century Romantics: the contrast with his close contemporary Alexander Skryabin (1872–1915) is striking, for in his relatively short life Skryabin advanced boldly into Expressionistic atonality. But, from the famous C sharp minor Prelude (1892) to the sumptuous slow section of the Paganini Variations (1934), it was expansive melody and sonorous tonal support that gained Rakhmaninov his great success. Those irritated by a lack of progressiveness and abrasiveness find him self-indulgently elegiac, all (polished) surface and no substance. Those more sympathetic find power and conviction, both on the relatively large scale of, in particular, the Second Symphony (1906–7) and the Second and Third Concertos (1900–01, 1909) and also in more miniature forms, such as the intensely expressive set of Preludes op. 32 (1910). Much of Rakhmaninov's appeal stems from his Russian roots, for although he never lived in his native land after the 1917 Revolution he was one of the very few composers talented enough to profit positively from the example of Tchaikovsky. He was also much interested in Russian liturgical chant, and it is these sources in particular that bring more than glibness and glitter to his best work. The lyrical themes of the Second Piano Concerto achieve an exalted eloquence that may approach the bombastic, but they skilfully stop on the brink. And it was perhaps the intensity and economy of chant that led him to shun the worst excesses of padding and protraction, even in his largest works.

There was nevertheless rather more of opulence than austerity about Rakhmaninov's music, due mainly to the absence of those more radical types of harmonic organization whose lack of large-scale perspectives forced many more progressive composers into economy and brevity: Skryabin is a case in point, a composer whose sheer breadth of response to different aspects of nineteenth-century

Romanticism provoked his own transformation from late Romantic into avant-garde Expressionist. Karol Szymanowski (1882–1937) is an equally interesting case, whose difficulties in escaping from the clutches of German influences – predominantly Richard Strauss – led him through a gamut of styles, from 'pure' Romanticism, late Romanticism and Impressionism to nationally-inspired Neoclass-icism in the 1920s. But it is the music of Jean Sibelius (1865–1957) that tests more effectively than any of these the elasticity and logic of terms like Romantic. Clearly enough, Sibelius progressed from an early style in which Romantic influences, notably Tchaikovsky, were very evident towards a much more personal, occasionally austere language whose affirmations of fundamental tonal principles – as in the glowing pages of the Symphony no. 7 or the bleak Nordic evocations of *Tapiola* – seem to echo both the heroic tone and the programmatic intensity of 'authentic' Romanticism. Alternatively, Sibelius's evident rejection of the Wagnerian invitation to ever more richly ramified expansion, an invitation which some historians see as doing more than any other development to promote the collapse of tonality and with it that of coherent musical discourse, can be read as evidence of a rejection of the essentials of Romanticism itself. Nevertheless, the very great differences between the tone of Sibelius's last works, or

51 The pensive northerner. Sibelius in 1934, eight years after completing *Tapiola*, his last surviving major work.

those of a contemporary, Carl Nielsen, and the genuinely Neoclassical music of the 1920s suggest that to deny such music a direct link to the Romantic tradition (or at least to its non-Wagnerian side) is, to say the least, misguided.

It cannot be denied that Skryabin and Szymanowski, as well as Schoenberg, Berg, Janáček, and a multitude of other composers, good and bad, lived out that transition from Romanticism to something else that is the story of twentieth-century music much more wholeheartedly than did either Sibelius or Nielsen. As a result, the most consistently Romantic twentieth-century composers have usually proved to be the most conservative, if not by that same token invariably the least interesting. As already suggested, Soviet Russia has offered a special, and specially ironic case, of Romantic tone surviving (and overpowering what might otherwise have become Expressionist or Neoclassical tendencies) in the major works of Shostakovich, the later Prokofiev (notably the Symphony No. 6) and others – and persisting into such relatively recent works as the far from life-affirming Piano Quintet (1976) by Alfred Schnittke, its haunting ending highly Romantic in its in-turned depth of personal feeling.

In England there is the equivocal case of Benjamin Britten (1913–1976), whose subject-matter and technique seem to owe so much to nineteenth-century traditions, yet whose style is ultimately too bound up with twentieth-century features derived from Ravel, Prokofiev and Stravinsky (as well as the pre-Romantic Purcell) to conform with any certainty to Romantic criteria. William Walton (1902–83) is a stronger candidate, his concertos and symphonies marking a more decisive retreat from the modernism of his youth and making a success of the difficult task of giving a personal slant to forms and features of style which are not in themselves original. Among younger British composers, the connection to Romantic traditions of Nicholas Maw, Robin Holloway and Colin Matthews is especially strong and fruitful.

In America the most successful and most maligned modern Romantic was Samuel Barber (1910–81), though many might wish to propose Leonard Bernstein or Gian Carlo Menotti as a more obvious representative of a conservatism dedicated to the warmly lyrical and passionately lively. In any case there is a clear distinction to be made between such a style and the kind of intentionally anonymous imitation of nineteenth- or early-twentieth-century styles sometimes termed 'new' (or neo-) Romanticism. The American George Rochberg (b. 1918) declared in the early 1960s that 'after abstractionism' comes the 'new romanticism', and by 1972 he was composing, in his String Quartet no. 3, in a style whose strongest links were with Brahms and Mahler. To many critics – and not a few fellow-composers – such a strategy of seemingly calculated anonymity, which at the same time shuns any identification with those contemporary idioms most widely regarded as valid and vital, represents a denial of creativity, however poignant and well-taken as a comment on the general cultural consequences of prevailing obsessions with novelty and originality. And even when a composer's Neoromanticism takes the form of a generalized conservatism whose main points of reference are late Romantic, rather than the deliberate cultivation of stylistic identity with any particular late Romantic master, it would seem abundantly clear that such Neoromanticism still awaits a figure comparable in mastery and personality to Neoclassicism's Stravinsky.

Certainly, it is difficult to claim that any of those composers who remained, or became, Romantics after 1920 have yet challenged in inventiveness or originality those who were never Romantic in the first place, or those who, having grown out of Romanticism, retained something of its eloquence and aspiration while relating more essentially to the post-Romantic world. The twilight of Romanticism has been long and eventful, nor is it over yet; indeed, some might argue that it has proved a northern, midsummer twilight which even now is being transformed into the new dawn of true Neoromanticism. If so, the problems of defining this are too complex, too unrealistic and too subject to rapid change, to be usefully tackled here.

The twentieth century may be, and may remain, predominantly anti-Romantic: but in its late stages it is still possible for composers to express an intimate familiarity with, and passionate allegiance to, the techniques, ideals, and even the idioms of the nineteenth century. Romanticism, it seems, is set to remain a permanent feature of serious music; it has already escaped the confines of its nineteenth-century flowering, and, with its survival, the post-Romantic age is itself the richer.

Abraham, Gerald, *Chopin's musical style* (London, 1939)
——, *A hundred years of music* (4th edn, London, 1974)
——, 'The apogee and decline of Romanticism: 1890–1914', in *The New Oxford History of Music*, X, *The Modern Age (1890–1960)* (London and New York, 1974)
Artz, Frederick B., *From Renaissance to Romanticism: trends in style in art, literature and music* (Chicago, 1962)
Ashbrook, William, *Donizetti and his operas* (Cambridge, 1982)
Banfield, Stephen, 'The Artist and Society', chap. I of N. Temperley, ed., *The Romantic age* (q.v.)
Barth, H., Mack, D. and Voss, E., compiled and ed., *Wagner, a documentary study*, tr. J. Ford and M. Whittall (London and New York, 1975)
Barzun, Jacques, *Classic, romantic and modern* (2nd rev. edn, New York, 1961)
Berlioz, Hector, *Evenings with the orchestra*, tr. and ed. J. Barzun (Chicago, 1956)
——, *The memoirs of Berlioz*, tr. and ed. D. Cairns (St Albans, 1970; New York, 1975)
Blume, Friedrich, *Classic and romantic music: a comprehensive survey*, tr. M. D. Herter Norton (New York, 1970; London, 1972)
Brown, Clive, *Louis Spohr, a critical biography* (Cambridge, 1984)
Brown, David, *Mikhail Glinka, a biographical and critical study* (London, 1974)
——, *Tchaikovsky, the early years: 1840–74* (London and New York, 1978)
——, *Tchaikovsky, the crisis years: 1874–8* (London and New York, 1982)
Budden, Julian, *The operas of Verdi* (3 vols) (London and New York, 1973; 1978; 1981)
——, *Verdi* (The master musicians) (London, 1985)
Burkholder, J. Peter, 'Brahms and twentieth-century classical music', in *19th-century music*, VIII, 1 (Summer 1984), pp. 75–82

Carner, Mosco, *Puccini, a critical biography* (2nd edn, London and New York, 1974)
——, *Hugo Wolf Songs* (BBC music guides) (London, 1982)
Chissell, Joan, *Schumann* (The master musicians) (London, 1977)
Chopin, Fryderyk, *Selected correspondence*, tr. and ed. A. Hedley (London, 1962)
Clapham, John, *Dvořák* (Newton Abbot and New York, 1979)
Conati, Marcello, *Interviews and encounters with Verdi*, tr. R. Stokes (London, 1984)
Cone, Edward T. ed., *Berlioz Fantastic Symphony* (Norton critical scores) (New York and London, 1971)
Cooke, Deryck, 'Bruckner', in *The New Grove Dictionary of Music and Musicians*, 3 (London and New York, 1980), pp. 352–71
Cooper, Martin, *French music from the death of Berlioz to the death of Fauré* (London, 1951)
Crosten, William L., *French grand opera, an art and a business* (New York, 1948; repr. 1972)
Dahlhaus, Carl, *Richard Wagner's music dramas*, tr. M. Whittall (Cambridge and New York, 1979)
——, *Between Romanticism and Modernism, four studies in the later nineteenth century*, tr. M. Whittall (California studies in nineteenth-century music) (Los Angeles, 1980)
——, *Realism in nineteenth-century music*, tr. M. Whittall (Cambridge and New York, 1985)
Davies, Lawrence, *César Franck and his circle* (London, 1970)
Dean, Winton, 'Donizetti's serious operas', in *Proceedings of the Royal Musical Association*, C, 1973–4, pp. 123–41
Deathridge, John and Dahlhaus, Carl, *The New Grove Wagner* (London and New York, 1984)
Delius, Frederick, *Delius, a life in letters*, comp. and ed. L. Carley (London, 1983)
Dent, Edward J., *The rise of romantic opera*, ed. W. Dean (Cambridge, 1976)

Forbes, Elliott, ed., *Beethoven Symphony No. 5 in C minor* (Norton critical scores) (New York and London, 1971)

Garden, Edward, *Balakirev, a critical study of his life and music* (London, 1967)

——, *Tchaikovsky* (The master musicians), rev. reprint (London, 1984)

Geiringer, Karl, *Brahms, his life and work*, tr. H. B. Weiner and B. Miall (3rd edn, Boston and London, 1963)

Hanslick, Eduard, *Music criticism 1846–99*, tr. and ed. H. Pleasants (rev. edn, New York and Harmondsworth, 1963)

Hepokoski, James A., *Giuseppe Verdi, Falstaff* (Cambridge opera handbooks) (Cambridge, 1983)

Honour, Hugh, *Romanticism* (London, 1979)

Horton, John, *Grieg* (The master musicians) (London, 1974)

Keller, Hans, 'Peter Ilyich Tchaikovsky', in *The Symphony*, ed. R. Simpson, I (Harmondsworth, 1967)

Large, Brian, *Smetana* (London, 1970)

Laudon, Robert T., *Sources of the Wagnerian synthesis, a study of the Franco-German tradition in nineteenth-century opera*, (Musikwissenschaftliche Studien, 2) (Munich, 1979)

Le Huray, Peter and Day, James, eds, *Music and aesthetics in the eighteenth and early nineteenth centuries* (Cambridge readings in the literature of music) (Cambridge, 1981)

Macdonald, Hugh, *Berlioz orchestral music* (BBC music guides) (London, 1969)

——, ed., *Berlioz. New edition of the Complete Works*, 2c, *Les troyens. Supplement* (Kassel, Basel, Paris, London, 1970)

——, *Berlioz* (The master musicians) (London, 1982)

McGann, Jerome J., *The Romantic ideology, a critical investigation* (Chicago and London, 1983)

Mahler, Gustav, *Selected letters . . . ed. by K. Martner*, tr. E. Wilkins, E. Kaiser and B. Hopkins (London and New York, 1979)

Medici, Maria, 'Lettere su *Re Lear*', in *Verdi, Bollettino dell' Istituto di Studi Verdiani*, I, 1960

Millington, Barry, *Wagner* (The master musicians) (London, 1984)

Mitchell, Donald, *Gustav Mahler, the early years* (London, 1958; rev. edn, London and Berkeley, 1980)

——, *Gustav Mahler, the Wunderhorn years* (London and Boulder, Colorado, 1976)

Newcomb, Anthony, 'Once more "between absolute and program music": Schumann's Second Symphony', in *19th-century Music*, VII, 3 (April 1984), pp. 233–50

Nochlin, Linda, *Realism* (Style and civilization) (Harmondsworth, 1971)

Orlova, Alexandra, *Musorgsky's days and works*, tr. and ed. R. Guenther (Studies in Russian music, 4) (Ann Arbor, 1983)

Pendle, Karin, *Eugène Scribe and French opera of the nineteenth century* (Studies in musicology, 6) (Ann Arbor, 1979)

Pestelli, Giorgio, *The age of Mozart and Beethoven*, tr. E. Cross (Cambridge, 1984)

Plantinga, Leon, *Schumann as critic* (Yale studies in the history of music, 4) (New Haven, 1967)

——, *Romantic music, a history of musical style in nineteenth-century Europe* (New York and London, 1984)

Praz, Mario, *The romantic agony* (London and New York, 1950)

Raby, Peter, *Fair Ophelia, a life of Harriet Smithson Berlioz* (Cambridge, 1982)

Radcliffe, Philip, *Mendelssohn* (The master musicians) (London, 1967)

Ridenour, Robert C., *Nationalism, modernism and personal rivalry in nineteenth-century Russian music* (Russian music studies) (Ann Arbor, 1981)

Ringer, Alexander L., 'Current Chronicle – St. Louis', in *Musical Quarterly*, 1961, p. 101 (a report of recent musical events, in particular the première of a work by George Rochberg)

Roberts, John H. (a review of 'Meyerbeer' in *The New Grove*), in *19th-century Music*, V, 2 (Fall 1981), pp. 161–3

Rosen, Charles, *The classical style* (London and New York, 1971)

——, and Zerner, Henri, *Romanticism and Realism, the mythology of nineteenth-century art* (London, 1984)

Rosen, David and Porter, Andrew, eds, *Verdi's Macbeth, a sourcebook* (Cambridge and New York, 1984)

Rosselli, John, *The opera industry in Italy from Cimarosa to Verdi; the role of the impresario* (Cambridge, 1984)

Rowell, Lewis, *Thinking about music, an introduction to the philosophy of music* (Amherst, 1983)

Rushton, Julian, *The musical language of Berlioz* (Cambridge studies in music) (Cambridge, 1983)

Schoenberg, Arnold, *Style and Idea* (2nd edn, London, 1975) (in particular the essays 'Franz

Liszt's Work and Being', pp. 442–7, and 'Brahms the Progressive' pp. 398–441)

Schuh, Willi, *Richard Strauss, a chronicle of the early years, 1864–98*, tr. M. Whittall (Cambridge, 1982)

Searle, Humphrey, *The music of Liszt* (2nd rev. edn, New York, 1966)

Strauss, Richard and Hofmannsthal, Hugo von, *The correspondence . . .*, tr. by H. Hammelmann and E. Osers (Cambridge, 1980)

Stravinsky, Igor, *Poetics of music* (New York, 1947)

Taruskin, Richard, *Opera and drama in Russia as preached and practiced in the 1860s* (Russian music studies, 2) (Ann Arbor, 1981)

Tchaikovsky, Peter Ilyich, *Letters to his family, an autobiography*, tr. G. von Meck, with additional annotations by P. M. Young (London and New York, 1981)

Temperley, Nicholas, ed., *The Romantic age, 1800–1914* (*The Athlone history of music in Britain*, 5) (London, 1981)

Vallas, Léon, *The theories of Claude Debussy, musicien français*, tr. M. O'Brien (London, 1929; repr. 1967)

Wagner, Richard, *Opera and Drama*, 1893 (first published 1851; quotations in the present book are from Wagner's *Prose Works*, tr. W. A. Ellis, London, 1892–8, vol. 3; however, some emendations have been made to the notoriously unsatisfactory translation)

——, *My life*, tr. A. Gray (Cambridge and New York, 1983)

Walker, Alan, *Franz Liszt, the virtuoso years, 1811–47* (London and New York, 1983)

Warrack, John, *Tchaikovsky* (London, 1973)

——, *Carl Maria von Weber* (2nd edn, Cambridge, 1976)

Watson, Derek, *Bruckner* (The master musicians) (London, 1975)

Weber, Carl Maria von, *Writings on music*, tr. M. Cooper, ed. J. Warrack (Cambridge, 1981)

Westernhagen, Curt von, *Wagner, a biography*, tr. M. Whittall (Cambridge, 1978)

Wheeler, Kathleen, ed., *German aesthetic and literary criticism; the Romantic ironists and Goethe* (Cambridge, 1984)

Winklhofer, Sharon, *Liszt's Sonata in B minor, a study of autograph sources and documents* (Studies in musicology, 29) (Ann Arbor, 1980)

Wolf, Hugo, *The music criticism . . .*, tr., ed. and annotated H. Pleasants (New York, 1978)

List of illustrations

1 C. D. Friedrich, *Ravine in the Elbsandstein Mountains*, c. 1823. *Kunsthistorisches Museum, Vienna*

2 J. Martin, *Manfred on the Jungfrau*, 1837. *City Museum and Art Gallery, Birmingham*

3 Rossetti, Lithograph of *Barricades in Milan, 19 March 1848*. *Archivio Fotografico, Comune di Milano*

4 Illustration of the Wolf's Glen scene from *Der Freischütz* by Weber. *Illustrated London News*, 23 March 1850. *Royal Opera House Archives*

5 J. Cawse, Portrait of Weber, 1829. *Royal College of Music*

6 M. von Schwind, *A Schubert Evening at Spaun's*, c. 1860. *Historisches Museum der Stadt Wien*

7 Wood engraving of Fingal's Cave c. 1850

8 Engraving, *Concert in the Leipzig Gewandhaus*, 1845. *Bildarchiv Preussischer Kulturbesitz*

9 J.-J. B. Laurens, Portrait of Schumann, October 1853. *Musée Duplessis, Carpentras*

10 Sir E. Landseer, Sketch of Paganini, c. 1831. *City of Manchester Art Galleries*

11 Contemporary lithograph of Bellini's *La Sonnambula*. *Royal Opera House Archives*

12 G. Pasta as Anna Bolena, engraving by H. Dupont. *The Harold Rosenthal Collection*

13 Caricature of Donizetti, from *Panthéon Charivarique*, 1840, Paris. Photo: *Bertarelli Collection, Milan*

14 Lithograph cartoon by Ghemant of Antoine (Adolphe) Sax, 1862. *Royal College of Music*

187

15 Engraving of the Coronation scene from Meyerbeer's *Le Prophète*, 1849. *Collection Viollet, Paris*
16 Berlioz's autograph score of the Dies Irae from the *Grande messe des morts*, 1837. *Bibliothèque de Conservatoire, Paris*
17 Caricature by G. Doré, *Concert of the Société Philharmonique in the Jardin d'Hiver* in Paris, *Le Petit Journal pour Rire*, Paris, 1856. Bibliothèque Nationale, Paris
18 G. Courbet, Portrait of Berlioz, 1860. Musée du Louvre, Paris. Photo: *Giraudon*
19 Chopin, Variations, op. 2 on Mozart's *Là ci darem la mano* from *Don Giovanni*. Holograph of the fifth variation. *Pleyel Collection, Paris*
20 E. Delacroix, *Portrait of Chopin*, 1838. Musée du Louvre, Paris. Photo: *Bulloz*
21 Bithorn, Silhouette of Wagner and Liszt
22 K. Lehmann, Portrait of Liszt, 1839. Musée Carnavalet, Paris. Photo: *Lauros-Giraudon*
23 *Liszt conducting the première of his oratorio St Elisabeth in Budapest, August 1865. Illustrated London News*, London, 9 September 1865. *Royal College of Music*
24 E. B. Kietz, Portrait of Wagner, Paris 1840/42. *Richard-Wagner-Gedenkstätte, Bayreuth*
25 Photograph of Wagner, February/March 1860 by Petit et Trinquart, Paris. *Richard-Wagner-Archiv, Bayreuth*
26 Wagner, page 389 of the autograph score of *Die Walküre* (Act III), 1856. *Richard-Wagner-Archiv, Bayreuth*
27 M. Brückner, setting for Act III of Cosima Wagner's 1886 production of *Tristan und Isolde* at Bayreuth. *Richard-Wagner-Gedenkstätte, Bayreuth*
28 Setting for Act III in Wieland Wagner's 1966 production of *Tristan und Isolde*. *Bildarchiv-Bayreuther Festspiele, photo: Lauterwasser*
29 Portrait of Verdi, *c*. 1843. *Museo Teatrale alla Scala, Milan*
30 A. Cassioli, *The Battle of Legnano*, 1860. Galleria d'Arte Moderna, Florence. Photo: *Mansell-Alinari Collection*
31 G. and P. Bertoja's set design for the first production of *Rigoletto* by Verdi, Venice, 1851. *Biblioteca Correr, Venice*
32 'Ape' (C. Pellegrini) lithograph of *Verdi*, published in *Vanity Fair*, London, 1879

33 I. Y. Repin, Portrait of Glinka, 1887. *Novosti Press Agency*
34 Title page of Balakirev's *Islamey*, revised edition, 1902
35 Photograph of Musorgsky, 1870s. Royal College of Music
36 Photograph of the world première of *Sleeping Beauty* by Tchaikovsky in January 1890 at the Maryinsky Theatre, St Petersburg. *Royal Opera House Archive*
37 Photograph of Tchaikovsky *c*. 1890. *Novosti Press Agency*
38 *Barricade in the Old Town, Prague, June, 1848*, from *Leipziger Illustrirte Zeitung*, Leipzig, 1848
39 Title page of Smetana's piano arrangement of *Vltava* from *Má Vlast*, revised edition, 1902, published by Urbanek, Prague. *Royal College of Music*
40 M. Švabinský, pencil drawing of Dvořák. Museum of Czech Music, Prague. Photo: *Dilia, L. Neubert*
41 E. Munch, programme for Ibsen's *Peer Gynt*, Paris, 1896. From G. Schiefler, *Verzeichnis des Graphischen Werks Edvard Munchs bis 1906*, Berlin, 1907
42 Photograph of Elgar by C. Grindrod, Malvern, 1903. *Royal College of Music*
43 Photograph of the Garden scene in the 1864 production of Gounod's *Faust* at Covent Garden. *Royal Opera House Archives*
44 W. Nowak, *Music Room in Brahms's Viennese Apartment*, 1904. *Historisches Museum der Stadt Wien*
45 Photograph of Brahms by M. Fellinger, 1896. *Historisches Museum der Stadt Wien*
46 Photograph of Bruckner, 1894. *Österreichische Nationalbibliothek, Vienna*
47 C. von Wagner, Portrait of Wolf, 1902. *Historisches Museum der Stadt Wien*
48 Photograph of Richard Strauss, 1890s. *Royal Opera House Archives*
49 E. Orlick, etching of Mahler, 1902. *Royal College of Music*
50 Poster of 1910 for Puccini's opera *La fanciulla del West*. *Royal College of Music*
51 Photograph of Sibelius, 1934. *Kustannusosakeyhtiö Otava, Helsinki*

Index

*Principal references are shown in
bold type and references to
illustrations in italics.*

Abraham, Gerald 76–7
Adam, Adolphe 36
Agoult, Marie d' 85
Alkan, Valentin 160
Ashbrook, William 50, 53
Auber, Daniel 36, 44, 58, 100
Austria 14, 17, 24–30, 113, 147,
    163–73, 177–8

Bach, C. P. E. 11, 16
Bach, J. S. 10, 34, 37, 42, 158
Bakunin, Mikhail 98
Balakirev, Mily 131–4, *34*, 137
Baldini, Gabriele 119
Balfe, Michael William 153
ballet 139–40
Banfield, Stephen 153
Barber, Samuel 183
Barezzi, Margherita 112
Bartók, Béla 175
Bayreuth 96, 104–5, 141, 147,
    159, 160
Beethoven, Ludwig van 10,
    12–13, 16, 18–19, 25, 28–9,
    31–3, 37, 39–42, 44, 46, 58,
    61, 63–6, 74–5, 79–80, 83,
    86–7, 89–90, 99–100, 105,
    107, 129, 132, 135, 144,
    147, 148, 158–60, 164–6,
    168, 170, 177
Bellini, Vincenzo 36, **46–9**, *11*,
    50–51, 54, 74, 110
Benedict, Julius 153
Bennett, William Sterndale 37,
    152–3
Berg, Alban 17, 183
Berlioz, Hector 18, *32*, 35, 42,
    45–8, 50, **55–71**, *16–18*, 73,

79–80, 82, 85, 87, 89,
    90–91, 94, 98, 100–01,
    106–7, 110, 119, 131–2,
    138, 144, 155, 163, 171
Béatrice et Bénédict 71
La damnation de Faust 68–9
Roméo et Juliette 68
Les troyens 69–71
Bernstein, Leonard 183
Bertoja, G. and P. *31*
Bertini, Auguste 39
Berton, Henri-Montan 21
Berwald, Franz 149
Biedermeier 26–7
Bismarck, Otto von 164, 166
Bizet, Georges 13, 121, 125, 139,
    151, 157, 179
Boieldieu, Adrien 21
Boito, Arrigo 122–6
Bordes, Charles 160
Borodin, Alexander 132, 137
Bradshaw, Graham 126
Brahms, Johannes 13, 30, 41–2,
    79, 87, 90, 147, 149–51,
    154, **163–7**, *44*–5, 168–70,
    174, 177, 184
Britten, Benjamin 153, 177, 183
Bruckner, Anton 30, 90–91, 144,
    156, **167–70**, *46*, 171–2, 177
Brückner, Max 27
Budden, Julian 54, 124
Bull, Ole 150
Bülow, Hans von 103–4, 174
Burkholder, J. Peter 166

Carter, Elliott 124
Cassioli, Amos *30*
Cawse, John *5*
Chabrier, Emmanuel 159
chamber music 29, 33–4, 42,
    138, 142, 153, 158–60, 166,
    183, 184

Chateaubriand, René de 83
Chausson, Ernest 160
Cherubini, Luigi 21, 99, 164
Chopin, Fryderyk 25, 37–9, 50,
    57, **72–80**, *19–20*, 83, 87,
    107, 110, 155, 160
    piano music 76–8
Classicism 9–12, 16–18, 25,
    28–30, 33–5, 37–9, 61, 71,
    79–80, 129, 148, 164–6
Coleridge, Samuel Taylor 10
concerto 32–3, 41–2, 148, 150,
    154, 166
conducting 56, 62, 65
Cooke, Deryck 168–70
Cramer, Johann Baptist 152
Courbet, Gustave 13, *18*
Crosten, William L. 60
Cui, César 132
Czechoslovakia 141–9

Dahlhaus, Carl 13, 96
Dalayrac, Nicolas-Marie 21
Dargomïzhsky, Alexander
    133–4
Davies, Peter Maxwell 177
Dean, Winton 54
Debussy, Claude 13, 66–7, 70,
    154–5, 157, 159–61, 175
Delacroix, Eugène *20*
Delibes, Léo 119
Delius, Frederick 152–5
Döhler, Theodor von 39
Donizetti, Gaetano 36, 46–7,
    49–54, *13*, 55, 71, 79, 101,
    110
    Anna Bolena 50–52
    Maria di Rohan 53–4
    Torquato Tasso 52
Doré, Gustave *17*
Dresden 20, 24, 32, 98–9
Dukas, Paul 161

Duparc, Henri 159–60
Dvořák, Antonín 79, 141,
   145–9, 40

Eichendorff, Joseph von 40, 172
Elgar, Edward 152–4, 42
Elsner, Józef 73–4
Empfindsamkeit 11–12, 16
England 79, 152–5, 183
Expressionism 13, 93, 164, 175,
   177, 181–3

Faccio, Franco 122
Fauré, Gabriel 160–61
Fibich, Zdeněk 149
Field, John 37, 74, 152
Flaubert, Gustave 13
France 17, 21, 36, 55–80, 83–5,
   155–61
Franck, César 151, 158–61
Friedrich, Caspar David 1

Gade, Niels 149
galant style 11, 16
Gautier, Théophile 50
Gaveaux, Pierre 21
Gesamtkunstwerk 24, 58
Geyer, Ludwig 97
Gilbert, Henry 161
Giordano, Umberto 179
Glinka, Mikhail 130–34, 33
Gluck, Christoph Willibald 11,
   16, 17, 47, 56, 60–64, 66–7,
   70, 99
Goethe, Johann Wolfgang von
   9, 11, 25, 28, 40, 42, 61, 63,
   90, 172–3
Gogol, Nikolay 134
Gottschalk, Louis Moreau 161
Gounod, Charles 125, 152,
   155–8, 43, 180
Grétry, André-Ernest-Modeste
   21, 99
Grieg, Edvard 149–51, 41, 161
Griffes, Charles T. 161
Guilmant, Alexandre 161

Halévy, Jacques-Fromental 52,
   58–9, 65, 100
Handel, George Frideric 10, 34
Hanslick, Eduard 49, 81–2,
   94–5, 109, 127, 174–6

Hartmann, J. P. E. 150
Haydn, Joseph 10–13
Hegel, G. W. F. 10
Heine, Heinrich 17, 27, 40, 45,
   98
Heinrich, A. P. 161
Heller, Stephen 15
Henze, Hans Werner 177
Hepokoski, James 126
Herz, Henri 39, 74
Hiller, Ferdinand 37
Hoffmann, E. T. A. 10, 31, 44,
   72, 98
Holloway, Robin 183
Homer 70
Hugo, Victor 58, 89, 112
Hummel, Johann Nepomuk 74
Humperdinck, Engelbert 161,
   174
Hünten, Franz 39

Ibsen, Henrik 149–50
Impressionism 13, 93, 151, 160,
   182
Indy, Vincent d' 159–60
Italy 36, 45–54, 110–28, 130,
   179–81
Ives, Charles 162

Janáček, Leos 148, 183
Johnson, Samuel 10, 19

Kalkbrenner, Frédéric 39, 74
Keats, John 9
Keller, Hans 130
Kietz, E. B. 24
Klinger, F. M. 11

Lamennais, Félicité de 84
Landseer, Edwin 10
Lanner, Joseph 77
Laroche, Hermann 136–7
Lehmann, Henri 22
Leipzig 8, 36, 97, 149–50
leitmotif 24, 31, 44, 99, 106–7,
   131, 146
Lekeu, Guillaume 160
Leoncavallo, Ruggero 115, 122,
   179
Lesueur, Jean-François 61
Lewis, M. G. 65
Lied 17, 24–8, 40–41, 171–3

Liszt, Franz 25, 30, 39, 46, 50,
   56, 64–5, 70, 73, 78–9,
   81–94, 21–3, 96, 99, 101,
   107, 110, 131–2, 134, 138,
   142–4, 148, 155–60, 162–3,
   165–6, 171–2, 174
   Faust Symphony 90–91
   piano music 84, 86–9
   sacred music 91–4
   symphonic poems 89–90
Loder, Edward 153
Loewe, Carl 40–41
London 23, 86
Lortzing, Albert 44
Louis-Philippe, King of France
   78, 83
Ludwig II, King of Bavaria 103–4

MacCunn, Hamish 153
Macdonald, Hugh 68
MacDowell, Edward 161
McGann, Jerome J. 10
Mahler, Alma 176
Mahler, Gustav 9, 28, 149, 156,
   176–8, 49, 184
Manzoni, Alexander 121
Marschner, Heinrich 43–4, 99
Martin, John 2
Mascagni, Pietro 115, 122, 179
Massenet, Jules 125, 157–8, 160,
   180
Matthews, Colin 183
Maw, Nicholas 183
Mayr, J. S. 52
Méhul, Etienne-Nicolas 21–2,
   27, 99
Mendelssohn, Felix 32–6, 37,
   41–2, 57, 76, 89, 132, 149,
   152, 154, 156
   orchestral and instrumental
   music 33–5
   vocal music 36
Menotti, Gian Carlo 183
Mercadante, Saverio 46, 122
Meyerbeer, Giacomo 20, 46–7,
   52, 56–60, 15, 61, 65, 67,
   71, 98, 100, 102, 114, 119,
   121, 125, 134, 142, 155–6,
   160
Michelangelo Buonarotti 87
Milan, La Scala opera 50, 112,
   125

Moke, Camille 63
Monteverdi, Claudio 10
Mörike, Eduard 173
Moscheles, Ignaz 74, 149
Moscow 134, 141
Mozart, Wolfgang Amadeus 10,
    12–13, 16–17, 31, 33–4, 37,
    114, 137, 147, 163
Müller, Wilhelm 28
Murger, Henri 180
Musorgsky, Modeste 13–14, 132,
    134–7, 35

Nationalism 13, 129–51, 142, 161
Neoclassicism 35, 182–4
Neoromanticism 96, 184
New German School 65, 165
Newcomb, Anthony 41
Nicolai, Otto 44
Nielsen, Carl 183
Nietzsche, Friedrich 105, 157
Nordraak, Richard 150
Novák, Vitezslav 148
Novalis (Friedrich von
    Hardenberg) 10

Offenbach, Jacques 119
opera 25, 36, 92, 153, 174
    Czech opera 142–4, 146–7
    French opera 56–60, 69–71,
        155–61
    German opera 18–24, 31–2,
        42–4, 98–109, 176
    grand opera 46–7, 56–60, 100,
        102, 134, 156
    Italian opera 46–54, 110–28,
        179–81
    music drama 88, 101–9, 172
    opéra-comique 21, 44, 60, 65,
        71, 155, 157
    Russian opera 130–39
orchestra, instruments of 55

Pacini, Giovanni 122
Paganini, Nicolò 45–6, *10*, 57,
    61, 87
Paine, John Knowles 161
Paris 17–18, 37, 39, 50, 54,
    56–72, 75–8, 83–6, 96, 98,
    113, 118–20, 150, 155, 158
Parry, Charles Hubert Hastings
    153–4

Pasta, Giuditta *12*
Pearsall, Robert Lucas 152
Pellegrini, Carlo ('Ape') *32*
pianoforte 39, 78, 86
piano music 34–5, 38–40, 72–8,
    84–9, 132, 152, 181
Pierson, Henry Hugo 152
Ponchielli, Amilcare 122
Powell, John 161–2
Prague 21, 141–2, *38*, 146
Praz, Mario 9
programme music 12, 21, 82,
    132, 137, 138, 161
Prokofiev, Sergey 183
Puccini, Giacomo 13, 122, 157,
    179–81, *50*
Purcell, Henry 183
Pushkin, Alexander 136

Raff, Joachim 153
Rakhmaninov, Sergey 181
Ravel, Maurice 183
Realism 13, 96, 115, 117, 127,
    129, 133–6, 157, 179–80
Recio, Marie 63
Reicha, Antoine 101
Repin, I. Y. *33*
Ricci, Federico and Luigi 122
Rimsky-Korsakov, Nikolay
    132–3, 135, 137, 161
Roberts, John H. 61
Rochberg, George 184
Romani, Felice 52
Rosen, Charles 39
Rosselli, John 54
Rossini, Gioachino 25, 46–8,
    49–50, 56, 58, 74, 79, 87,
    100, 121
Rousseau, Jean-Jacques 21
Rubinstein, Anton 39, 131–2
Rubinstein, Nikolay 137
Rückert, Friedrich 40
Russia 130–41, 181, 183
    Russian Musical Society 131–2

sacred music 36, 92–3, 121–2,
    166, 168
St Petersburg 120, 131, 133, 139,
    141
Saint-Saëns, Camille 155–8
Saint-Simonism 84
Sand, George 72, 78

Sax, Antoine *14*
Sayn-Wittgenstein, Princess
    Carolyne de 70, 85–6, 106
Scandinavia 149–51, 182–3
Schelling, F. W. J. von 20–21
Schiller, Friedrich von 11, 28
Schlegel, K. W. F. 10, 20
Schmitt, Florent 161
Schnittke, Alfred 183
Schoenberg, Arnold 30, 81–2,
    90, 93, 109, 165, 175, 177,
    181, 183
Schola Cantorum 160
Schopenhauer, Arthur 95–6, 107
Schubert, Franz Peter 17, 22,
    24–30, 31–3, 37, 39–40, 61,
    74, 79, 86, 132, 147–8, 170,
    173, 177
    chamber music 29–30
    piano music 29–30
    symphonies 28–30
    operas 25
    songs 17, 25–8
Schumann, Clara 38, 76, 142,
    163
Schumann, Robert 12–13, 15,
    29, 32–4, **36–44**, 9, 50,
    54–5, 60, 66, 71, 76, 79–80,
    85, 87, 89–90, 107, 110,
    132, 134–5, 142, 149, 151,
    156, 158, 160, 163, 166, 172
    chamber music 42
    orchestral music 41–2
    piano music 38–40
    vocal music 40, 42
Schwind, Moritz von 6
Scribe, Eugène 57–60, 65, 70,
    98, 119
Sechter, Simon 168
Serov, Alexander 131–2
Shakespeare, William 61, 63,
    113, 120, 125–6
Shostakovich, Dmitri 177, 183
Sibelius, Jean 182–3, *51*
Simrock, music publishers 146
Skryabin, Alexander 181–3
Smetana, Bedřich **141–6**, *39*,
    148–9
Smithson, Harriet 63
Smyth, Ethel 153
Spaun, Joseph von 6
Spohr, Louis 21, **31–2**, 33, 36,

44–6, 49, 74, 99, 100
Spontini, Gaspare 47, 56, 58, 64,
  66, 87, 99
Stanford, Charles Villiers 154
Strauss, Johann, the elder 77
Strauss, Richard 25, 28, 77, 90,
  147, 153–4, 161, **174–6**, *48*,
  177, 182
Stravinsky, Igor 124, 137, 175,
  183–4
Strepponi, Giuseppina 114–15
Strindberg, August 149
Sturm und Drang 11–12, 16, 20
Suk, Josef 148–9
Suppé, Franz 164
Svendsen, Johan 149
symphonic poem 88–90, 143–4,
  156, 160, 174
symphony 14, 28–30, 33, 41, 64,
  68, 90–91, 129–30, 137–8,
  140–41, 147, 149, 156, 159,
  164–6, 167, 177–8
Szymanowski, Karol 182–3

Tchaikovsky, Piotr 129–32,
  137–41, *36–7*, 148, 150,
  156–8, 161, 174, 181–2
Thalberg, Sigismond 39
Thomas, Ambroise 180
Tieck, Ludwig 20
tone poem *see* symphonic poem

United States of America 146–7,
  161–2

Verdi, Giuseppe 13–14, 46, 52,
  54–5, 59–60, 66, 70–71, 79,
  87, 94, 101, **110–28**, *29–32*,
  136, 138, 140, 145, 151,
  154, 156–7, 160, 179
  Aida 119, 121–2

Un ballo in maschera 119–20
Don Carlos 118, 120–22, 125
Falstaff 71, 121, 124–8
La forza del destino 52, 54,
  118, 120, 122
Macbeth 113–14, 118
Nabucco 111–14
Otello 118, 121, 125–8, 157,
  179
Requiem 121–2
Rigoletto 112–18, 120
Simon Boccanegra 118–19, 125
La traviata 13, 110, 114–15,
  117–19
Il trovatore 114, 117, 120
Les vêpres siciliennes 118–19
verismo see Realism
Veron, Louis 58
Vienna 19, 24–5, 54, 61, 74, 83,
  141, 144, 149–50; 155,
  163–4
Vinje, Aasmund 151
Virgil 60–63, 70
Vogl, Johann Michael 6
Vogler, Georg Joseph 20

Wackenroder, W. H. 20
Wagner, Carl Friedrich 97
Wagner, Cosima 85, 103–5, 108
Wagner, Minna 98, 103–4
Wagner, Richard 12–13, 19, 22,
  24, 31–2, 36–7, 40, 42–4,
  47–50, 52, 54–5, 57–61,
  64–5, 70, 79, 81–3, *21*, 85,
  87–93, **94–109**, *24–8*, 110,
  112–15, 119–28, 132, 134–6,
  139–40, 143, 145–8, 151,
  153–4, 156–61, 163, 165–72,
  174, 182
  essays 97–8, 103, 105–6
  Faust Overture 89–90, 100

Der fliegende Holländer 32, 40,
  44, 98, 101–2
Götterdämmerung 126, 128
Lohengrin 22, 56, 85, 94, 98,
  101–2
Die Meistersinger 106, 108,
  122, 143
Parsifal 101, 105, 108–9, 126,
  128, 174
Das Rheingold 101, 104, 107–8
Rienzi 44, 98, 100–01, 123
Der Ring des Nibelungen 43,
  103–4, 107, 139, 178
Siegfried 22, 123
Tannhäuser 22, 32, 49, 85, 98,
  101–4
Tristan und Isolde 31, 90, 94,
  99, 108, *27–8*, 115, 120,
  123, 157, 159
Die Walküre 104–5, *26*, 107
Wagner, Siegfried 174
Wallace, Vincent 153
Walton, William 183
Weber, Carl Maria von **17–24**,
  5, 25, 27, 31–3, 36, 43–4,
  58, 66, 74, 90, 98–100, 107,
  114, 132, 135, 153
  Euryanthe 19, 22–3, 44, 99
  Der Freischütz 17–22, *4*, 74
  Oberon 23–4
  Silvana 20
Weimar 56, 70, 85, 88, 92, 99,
  141, 142, 156
Wesendonck, Mathilde 103, 115
Wesendonck, Otto 103
Wesley, Samuel Sebastian 152
Wolf, Hugo 12, 28, 31, 33,
  39–40, 82, 90–91, 94–6,
  144, 165, 169, **171–3**, *47*

Young Germany 97, 100